JOHN BROOKES'
NATURAL LANDSCAPES

JOHN BROOKES'
NATURAL LANDSCAPES

DK PUBLISHING, INC.

A DK PUBLISHING BOOK
PROJECT EDITOR Jennifer Jones
ART EDITOR Catherine MacKenzie
US EDITORS Mary Sutherland, Ray Rogers
PICTURE RESEARCHERS Mollie Gillard, Helen Fickling
PRODUCTION MANAGERS Kate Hayward, Meryl Silbert

MANAGING ART EDITOR Steve Knowlden
MANAGING EDITOR Ian Whitelaw

ILLUSTRATOR Gill Tomblin
SPECIAL PHOTOGRAPHY Howard Rice, Steven Wooster

First American edition, 1998
2 4 6 8 10 9 7 5 3 1

Published in the United States by DK Publishing, Inc.,
95 Madison Avenue, New York, New York 10016
Visit us on the World Wide Web at http://www.dk.com

Library of Congress Cataloguing-in-Publication Data
Brookes, John, 1933–
John Brookes' natural landscapes. -- 1st American ed.
p. cm.
Includes index.
ISBN 0–7894–1995–5
1. Natural landscaping. I. Title. II. Title: New natural
garden.
SB439.B66 1997   97–14827
635.95--DC21   CIP

Reproduced by Scanner Service srl., Italy
Printed and bound by Butler & Tanner in Great Britain

CONTENTS

AUTHOR'S FOREWORD

I GARDEN AT DENMANS, a sheltered spot five miles from the sea, close to the chalk downs of Southern England. The garden was started in the 1940s by the late Joyce Robinson, and from the beginning, her approach was very different from that of her contempories. Instead of establishing large formal flower borders, which were in vogue at the time, she decided to go for a more natural look. Working with rather than against the limitations of the location, she placed her plants in loose associations in the well-drained, gravelly soil typical of this region. Later, inspired by dry stream courses she had seen on vacation in Greece, she excavated and planted a dry stream bed. Here was planting in a wild way, albeit using introduced species, in a medium other than a cultivated bed. In the early 1980s I took over Joyce's garden, taking up the reins where she had left off. I had already experimented in small London gardens at replacing grass (which only becomes muddy in winter) with gravel and paved areas, and I warmed to her way of thinking. Since then, I like to think that my work at Denmans has remained true to the spirit in which the garden was established, but done in my own way. Recently, I have started to grow a wider range of native material, both shrubby and perennial. Although many of these are invasive, I am excited by their potential in terms of form and texture. I combine these with Mediterranean plant material, which likes the local well-drained, dryish soil, to create planting designs with which I am well pleased. My approach to the natural garden is to mix introduced species with the wild, rather along the lines of Piet Oudolf's garden in the Netherlands (see p.18). I prefer this approach – as opposed to one that is totally true to nature and creates an ecologically correct plant association for a given area – because it gives me more flexibility. Nevertheless, some stunning gardens are achieved taking the purist's line, as you will see in this book. Whatever approach you choose, I urge you to look to nature for your guide and consult your own understanding of your location – do this, and you cannot fail to achieve a garden that is in keeping with its setting.

JOHN BROOKES
Denmans, Spring 1998

A New Approach

Although there is nothing new about people's regard for the natural world, there is everything new about an approach to gardening that actively encourages nature into our gardens. What is meant by this, and how to go about creating a natural garden, are examined in the following chapters — from integrating the garden into the landscape so that it is truly in sympathy with its setting, to considering various design elements, including natural planting plans. In Part One, the natural approach to gardening is also put into a historical context, for there is much we can learn from early proponents of gardens inspired by nature.

THE NATURAL GARDEN

TRADITIONALLY, THE GARDEN was always regarded as an enclosure in which to create an exotic fantasy, far removed from what was happening naturally beyond its boundaries – to be sustained by endless cultivating, watering, and spraying. Inspired by the grand historical home and its garden, we have opted for a scaled-down version of gracious living, instead of a more natural, rural treatment in which the garden burgeons from the surrounding land to be part of its environment.

Is it necessary for the gardener to be at odds with nature in this way? I do not believe so, for there is a new approach we can take. Instead of pinning our aesthetic values solely on color and artifice, we can rediscover the natural elegance of our native plants; we can accept that our gardens should be of their place, with their own climate, soil, flora, fauna, and cultural traditions, and then design and plant them with this in mind. If we can celebrate the distinct and diverse glories of our countryside in this way, we will not continue to destroy its unique regional identity.

Wild wetland
A beautiful piece of "natural" wetland planting in Cambridgeshire, England, forms part of man-made fenland.

Woodland floor, *left*
Ferns drift in their natural habitat of deciduous woodland with fallen trees, thriving in semishade and damp soil rich in leaf litter.

Natural planting, *right*
Study the wild and you can develop some very satisfying garden plantings. Angelica, Scots thistle (Onopordum spp.), *and feverfew* (Tanacetum parthenium) *grow in my own garden in Sussex, England.*

Natural design inspiration
The swirling currents of water around rocks are simulated with a carefully raked sea of gravel in this Tofukuji temple kare sansui or "dry garden" in Kyoto, Japan.

Moss garden
The beauty of mosses, stone, and wood are perfectly realized in this Japanese garden.

Such a concept of gardening is not based on some sentimental notion about nature. It arises from a wish to do something practical about maintaining our disappearing habitats. We can start by using local materials for garden structures. We can introduce native plants, ideally grouped together as they would be in nature. Local materials and native and naturalized plants complement each other, and give us garden-makers a new sense of what is beautiful – a garden that is "organic," whole, and harmonious. By looking and learning from nature, we can encourage a broader diversity of wildlife to ensure a far healthier environmental balance.

This doesn't mean that we should allow nature to take over in the garden. The more natural the approach, the stronger the basic design should be, or the garden can slip into chaos. The aim should be to create a working partnership with nature, rather than trying to conquer it and mold it. But nor does it mean that the natural route is necessarily easier in terms of garden management. As the American landscape architect Jens Jensen commented, "Skillful maintenance is as necessary to natural plantings as to formal ones."

Working with nature

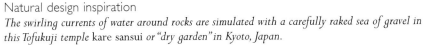

The Japanese are absolute masters at creating a harmonious working partnership with nature, in this case using rocks with water and plantings, all in total sympathy with each other.

The Japanese influence

Of course, there is nothing totally new about the idea that the gardener should embrace and celebrate nature. The Japanese have always looked to nature to teach them about beauty, and gardens are seen as an art form in which the creator attempts to capture the essence of that natural beauty.

Over the centuries, the Japanese have evolved an approach that extracts the essential elements of a landscape and reinterprets them in a stylistic shorthand. The harmonies of still pools, rushing streams, and mountain peaks are evoked on a smaller scale in the garden by water features, gravel surfacings, and stone groupings, which are combined with stylized massings of trees and shrubs. Once the idea is understood, the composition can be pared down to a bowl arrangement or even a single flower without destroying the imagery.

The principles and techniques of this refinement in garden design, the bold use of pebbles and boulders, and above all the integration of house with garden had a profound influence on both architecture and garden design in the West during the early twentieth century – and they are still relevant now to the natural gardener. The Japanese point to a way of attaining inner peace through the re-creation of nature, bringing a traditional art astonishingly close to the needs of the modern world.

The Romantic approach
Probably painted in the early 20th century, this picture by A.C. Strachan epitomizes the nostalgia many people still feel for what might now seem like the lost golden age of the simple, rural cottage lifestyle.

The traditional cottage garden

In the West, our naturalistic traditions stem from the original cottage garden; here, the nature of the site and the local way of life dictated which indigenous plants were grown, but it was a garden essentially devoted to providing food for the table. As well as growing fruit and vegetables, cottagers might also keep chickens and a pig. Trees on surrounding land were often coppiced for firewood and furniture-making. Herbs were grown for medicinal use, for cooking, dyeing, and for strewing on the beaten-earth floor of the house.

Every bit of land was brought into production by the cottager; flowers purely for decorative effect were not included, simply because they were not useful, although lilies may have been grown for use in church ceremonies and festivals. However, by the late nineteenth century, as communications improved and lifestyles changed, and cross-permutations of plants became more common, the decorative cottage garden began to emerge.

Romancing nature

The eighteenth century saw the emergence of the artistic movement in Europe known as Romanticism. Through their art, the Romantics — writers, poets, and painters — espoused the sanctity of nature in its pristine, untamed state. This concept was carried forward by the Arts and Crafts movement, and through the work of the plantswoman Gertrude Jekyll (1843–1932), whose plantings "in a wild way" were revolutionary at the time, even though her garden was still heavily cultivated. Many watercolor artists at the turn of the nineteenth century portrayed the garden in an idealized, romantic light, and it is this imagery that has provided the prototype for many of today's gardens. We are still trapped, I believe, in the afterglow of this so-called Golden Era.

Change has come about not so much through innovative ideas as through such pragmatic considerations as labor shortages and an abundance of gadgets and garden machinery. Gardens have loosened up, and many larger gardens now feature areas of rougher grass and wild plantings. Borders are still cultivated, but perennials have made an enormous return to popularity, reducing the tyranny of the exotic, and fragile, annual. Shrubs too are gaining in importance. This romantic style has been extolled by a number of contemporary plantswomen. The nurseries and gardens of naturalist Nancy Goodwin and the British commercial grower Beth Chatto are a

A contemporary vision, right
Perhaps not so far removed visually from the cottage garden of old, this magical planting in England by Beth Chatto takes a natural approach, based on the influences of her own time and her own specific site.

constant source of inspiration. In the United States, many gardeners are embracing a more natural approach. Hectic lifestyles and limited leisure time mean fewer hours available for labor-intensive landscapes, and extremes of climate encourage the use of native plants.

Early influences

To trace the development of the true natural garden we must look elsewhere, and first to the Danish landscape architect Jens Jensen (1860–1951), who emigrated to the United States in 1884. He felt the only way forward was for humans to operate as part of their environment. "We shall never produce an art of landscaping that is worthwhile until we have learned to love the soil and the beauty of our homeland," he wrote in 1939. Jensen's approach to ecology was also refreshingly tolerant. "Human beings," he stated, "are part of the environment, with needs as valid as those of plants and animals."

Jensen's poetic, ecologically sensitive interpretations of the great prairies and glacial hills of the Midwest offered timely inspiration to Americans everywhere. His theories were also hugely important in the development of the park system in Chicago and in garden designs in its northern suburbs. He made frequent excursions to wild woods and meadows so that he could base his native plant compositions on an accurate understanding of the ecological processes that he observed.

The Dutch movement

Jensen's technique of bringing the country into the city would have been well understood by the Dutch biologist Jac Thijsse (1865–1945), who was conscious that existing gardens and parks in his native Netherlands failed to give people any experience of their natural environment. In 1925, Thijsse created a natural garden in Bloemendaal near Haarlem, following the design of the landscape architect Leonard Springer. It contained a small woodland, a pond and marsh, a piece of heathland, a dune landscape, and a field of rare edible weeds. It was intended that the garden should be visited so that its message – that it is vital that we should understand and appreciate our natural environment – would spread.

Thijsse went on to evolve a park, now named after him, south of Amsterdam, in the form of a series of woodland glades, each one creating a landscape picture. There the public has been educated about wild flora and made aware that the natural environment is something we cannot replace or do without.

Thijsse was also aware that wild gardens need careful maintenance to remove anything unwanted. He developed what he called the phytosociological garden, in which characteristic habitats and plant communities of the surrounding area were re-created. In one such garden, fertile topsoil was removed to reveal sand dunes, since the location was near the North Sea coastline. The

Influential designers, *left and above*
Jens Jensen's natural planting in Lincoln Memorial Garden, Illinois (left) includes a stone circle meeting area. In the Netherlands, Jac Thijsse paralleled Jensen's work; his natural park (above) was completed in 1925.

Woodland walk, *above*
Ferns flourish along both sides of a woodland path in Thijsse Park, Amsterdam, Netherlands. Thanks to Jac Thijsse's vision, visitors today can experience a range of protected natural habitats.

Managed associations, above
To the uninitiated, these plantings by Dutch designer Piet Oudolf are not so far removed from the time-consuming herbaceous border. In fact, these are managed plant associations rather than a cultivated garden, taking their inspiration from the wild landscape rather than from the theories of Gertrude Jekyll.

Natives and exotics, right
Ton ter Linden associates plants native to his particular habitat in the north of the Netherlands with introduced species to create stunning arrangements. Another vital element of his compositions is lent by his artist's eye.

landforms were further exaggerated, and drainage ditches, shallow lakes, and varied shorelines were constructed. The result was a series of dune landscapes, which eventually required only annual mowing of grass and reeds and an occasional thinning of trees.

Nature's mosaics

Dutch garden design in recent years has been heavily influenced by "the natural way." The emphasis is on natural planting patterns in the form of a series of bold mosaics, with careful plant selection providing an overall cohesion. The new "liberating" principle of plant management is to reduce intervention by the gardener and to permit, to some extent, spontaneous self-seeding, turning a blind eye to unruly edges and overgrown corners of the garden. Nature is allowed to breathe.

Piet Oudolf is one of the nurserymen/garden designers of this movement. His design philosophy is that the form and structure of plant associations are more important than color, which he uses purely to create atmosphere. His designs aim for a long season of interest and continuity of balance, with low carpeting bulbs used to supplement spring effects. When summer flowers are over, the plants' appeal extends well into autumn, making maximum use of their forms. His style leans heavily toward the wild landscape, and the effects he achieves truly reflect nature's rich tapestry.

An artist's eye

Ton ter Linden is a contemporary of Oudolf, a painter-plantsman with an approach to gardening that can only be described as impressionistic. "I see each border as a watercolor; light is all important," he says. "I like to see tall, airy plants so that you can see the light fall through them." Ton ter Linden's plantings are indeed wonderfully transparent, with strong colors being toned down by silver and gray foliage woven through them. Ornamental grasses are used in almost every border, shimmering in the sunlight and lending an airiness to his garden, which is in the northern Drenthe region of the Netherlands.

Although I find these new Dutch plantings exciting, to my eye they lack punctuation in the form of evergreen material. In the Netherlands, evergreens are used mainly to shield the garden from prevailing winds along its borders, not as a decorative feature. The message is to look and learn from others' experience, and then adapt it to suit your own situation and taste.

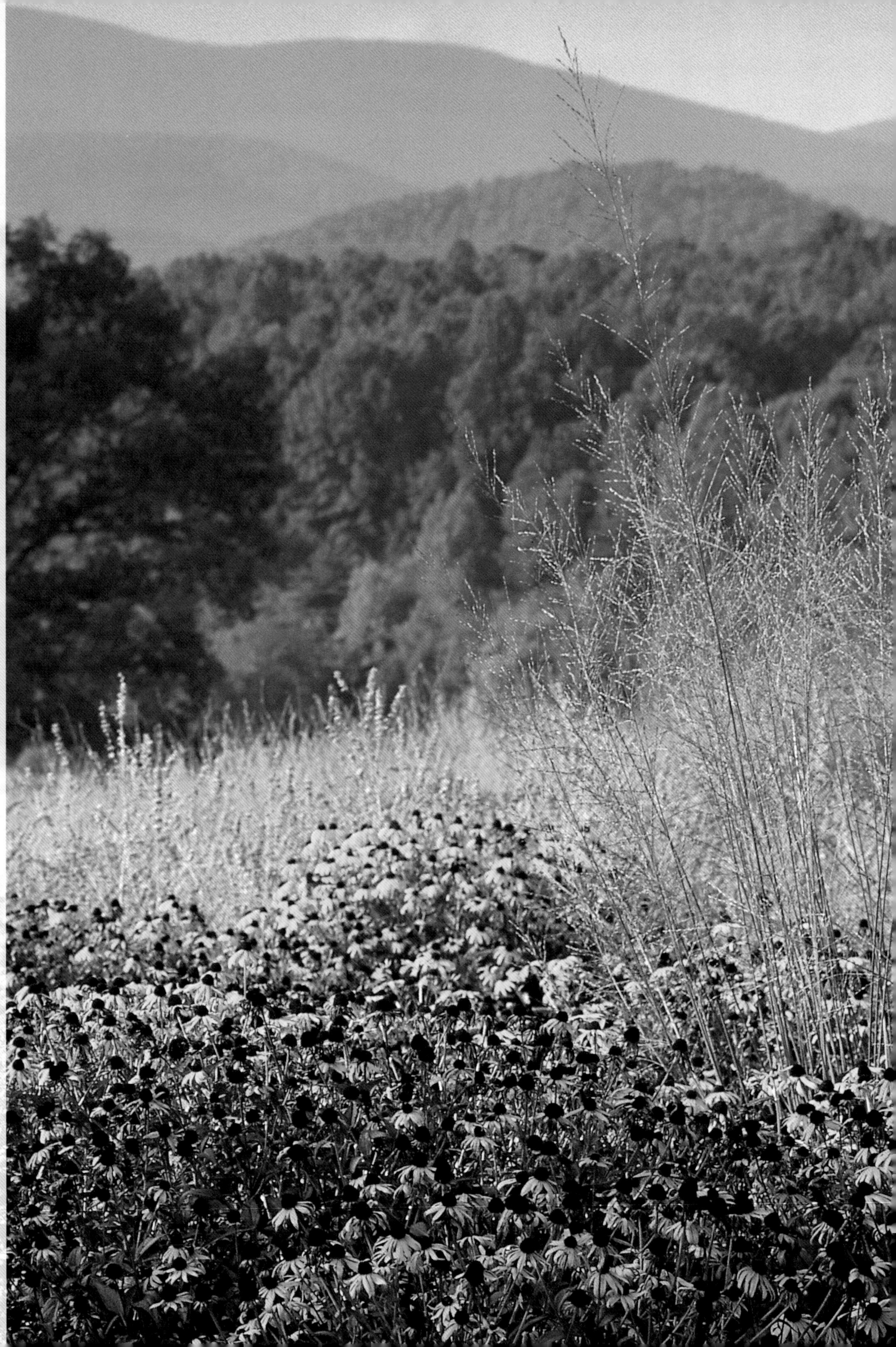

Informal gardens by design, *left, right, and far right*
A corner of a Wolfgang Oehme and James van Sweden garden in Virginia
(left) is planted with yellow coneflowers (Ratibida pinnata); en masse,
their contours echo those of the landscape beyond. In another garden
designed by Oehme and van Sweden (right and far right), informal
planting overlies a strong design in both summer and winter. Grasses,
which are cut down in spring, feature heavily in these massings.

New world, new gardens

The natural gardening movement in the United States
has burgeoned in recent years. More and more
traditional gardeners are joining its ranks as concern for
disappearing species of wildlife grows. Along with an
increasing awareness of the importance of using regional
plants, there is a desire to work in sympathy with the
landscape. It is this "essence of place" that the
contemporary work of landscape architects Wolfgang
Oehme and James van Sweden best portrays. They
overlay their designs with native and non-native material
planted nature's way, in bold swaths that are in harmony
with the scale of the landscape.

The new plantings of Oehme and van Sweden, and of
Piet Oudolf and Ton ter Linden, came as a liberating
revelation to me. While the diehard school advocates
ecologically correct plant associations for a specific area,
here was another approach, one that mixed introduced
species with wild ones.

Elsewhere in the world, in Germany, Rosemarie
Weisse of Westpark, Munich, and Urs Walser of Stuttgart
have pioneered wild meadow-planting design. Their

spectacular displays couldn't be further removed from
the enriched traditional border style and are planted on
poor, stony soil that the Germans call "steppe."

Australia, too, has seen interest in bringing native
plants into the garden to use either mixed with exotic
species or on their own. The British gardener, on the
other hand, has been slow to take up a natural approach
to landscape design or to apply ecological principles.
Where efforts have been made, the use of vegetation has
lacked both the spontaneity and the control of the Dutch
model. The new approach continues to be anathema to
the horticultural lobby, which finds it too far removed
from the romantic ideas of nature that we hold so dear.

The way forward

To the gardener new or old I would say, to quote the
eighteenth-century poet Alexander Pope, "Consult the
genius of the place in all," and then work with it. This
way a new garden type can emerge, one that is truly of
its place. I would like to see local materials come to the
fore, with local artists and designers offering services
that are "site specific." By the same token, growers and
garden centers might allocate areas to native plants of
their soil and region, and not just to wildflowers *per se*.

We are all the guardians of this planet during our
short lives, and we can all care for our own small patch;
cumulatively these patches make up a vast amount of
land. If our gardens can develop more naturally, in tune
with their specific place, we will contribute toward a far
healthier habitat for future generations to inherit.

Essence of place, *left*
Meadow plantings by Rosemarie Weisse in Munich, Germany, use only
those plants that grow in their natural, unimproved habitats.

WHAT IS NATURAL GARDENING?

THE ESSENCE OF NATURAL gardening is working with nature rather than struggling to master it or to change it. You therefore need to know as much as possible about the conditions in your garden – including climate, altitude, soil type, and prevailing winds – and about the kinds of plants that would grow there if it were left uncultivated. What happens naturally on the surface of the earth has largely to do with what goes on beneath it. Complex interactions of climate working upon geology, water resources, and latitude together produce the world's soil types and, as an extension of this, the types of plants and animals that thrive upon it.

For the natural gardener, the challenge is to exploit what happens naturally – taking advantage of the site's existing conditions – while managing it in such a way as to create a satisfying, aesthetically pleasing, and well-designed garden. You can learn a great deal from looking at the surrounding landscape, too: there will be distinctive natural features and land profiles, and typical local styles and materials as well as native plants. Echoing the characteristics of your immediate environment will help you create a garden that looks both natural and in tune with its context.

Woodland garden, *right*
In this Pennsylvania garden by A.E. Bye, native plants and natural rock formations are harmoniously combined in a woodland corner.

Prairie lands, *left*
The relationship between the pattern of harvested grain fields and land contours could give the new gardener clues to planting designs in relation to levels.

A Mediterranean setting, *right*
Lucky the gardener with such a backdrop. Despite the aridity of the foreground, there is still a wealth of native vegetation to be exploited.

A GLOBAL VIEW

The interaction of climate, geology, water resources, and latitude produces the Earth's soil types, its flora and fauna and, where it is managed, its land patterns too. There are fourteen major ecological regions – called "biomes" – distributed across five major climatic regions. Each biome is a distinct regional climatic type with its own flora and fauna. These biomes describe what the world would be like if we had not altered it. Forests once covered three-quarters of the land surface, with rainforest alone containing one-third of the world's plant matter. Europe and much of the eastern United States was covered in temperate broadleaved forest, before human incursions into it with agricultural and industrial development. If you leave a piece of land uncultivated for any length of time, the original type of vegetation will regenerate itself, first as pioneer plants, then herbs and grasses, shrubs, and (ultimately) trees.

Your piece of the earth

We do not garden in a vacuum. Your particular plot is part of a landscape, a region, a landmass, a climatic zone, all of which affect its conditions and what you can grow. Of key importance is the type of habitat and the setting of your site. Whether it is by the sea, in a town, on marshland, or in semi-desert, there will be characteristic factors that affect how you can best plan and plant your garden. This book covers the principal types of setting with which most gardeners are faced, and provides strategies for making the most of the conditions that are typically found in a given locale: Coastal, Temperate, Woodland, Wetland, Grassland, Dryland, Mediterranean, Tropical or Subtropical, and City. It may be that more than one category applies to your garden – coastal and temperate, for example – and a city garden may be in any one of them.

COASTAL
Good views and mild temperatures may make up for strong, salt–laden winds and poor soil in coastal regions (see pp. 58–67).

WETLAND
Wetlands such as bog areas, pools, and streams are rich habitats ideal for lush plant growth and varied wildlife (see pp. 102–115).

MEDITERRANEAN
The sunny, semiarid conditions found in Mediterranean regions suit a wide range of herbs and shrubs that need little water (see pp. 140–151).

TEMPERATE
Temperate regions offer conditions that suit a wide range of plants, with relatively mild temperatures and sufficient rainfall (see pp. 68–87).

WOODLAND
Many bulbs, ferns, and other shade–tolerant plants will grow beneath the canopy of deciduous trees (see pp. 88–101).

GRASSLAND
In natural grassland, such as prairies or pampas, grasses grow along with wildflowers, and trees are scarce or absent (see pp. 116–127).

DRYLAND
In dryland and desert regions, a range of extraordinary drought–tolerant plants thrive in unpromising conditions (see pp. 128–139).

TROPICAL
The heat and humidity in the tropics and subtropics make for rapid plant growth, creating a junglelike effect (see pp. 152–161).

CITY
Urban gardens typically offer sheltered sites, with milder temperatures, modified by the concentration of buildings (see pp. 162–183).

ASSESSING YOUR SITUATION

There is a frequent wail of "Oh, nothing will grow on my clay/chalky/waterlogged soil." What is meant is that nothing exotic will grow. The reply must be: "But you are surrounded by lush woodland or verdant countryside. Don't do anything and something *will* grow." Work with what you have — why fight it? Central to this approach is an assessment of your site, including its orientation, rainfall, prevailing winds, and locale. Unlike conventional gardens, many natural ones are most distinctive when strongly tempered by the elements — on a windy site, a boggy one, in a desert setting, or by the ocean — where they represent not only a definite plant community but a clear vernacular style as well. When you look at a landscape, you see the influence of many natural factors — geology, soil, weather — and of cultivation and management. There may be various specific habitats within this — mixed-species thickets, rolling hills, coppiced woods, marshes. These are the areas where you may study native plants, their associations, and their growing habits.

Winter field patterns

Clay-tiled roofs

Church

The view from above
An aerial photograph of the immediate area will elaborate upon much of the information already given by your large-scale map, showing colours, materials, and three-dimensional forms and thus giving you a stronger sense of the local characteristics.

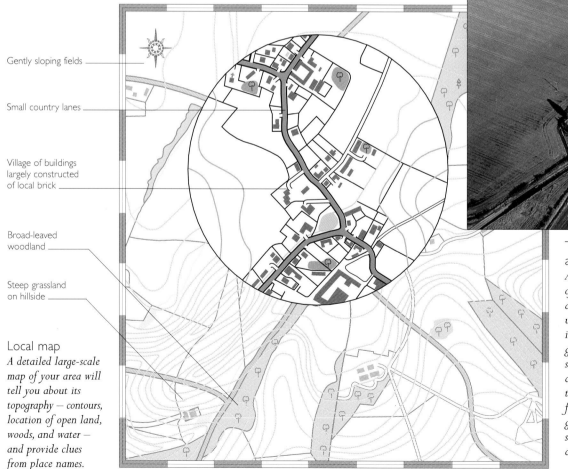

Gently sloping fields

Small country lanes

Village of buildings largely constructed of local brick

Broad-leaved woodland

Steep grassland on hillside

Local map
A detailed large-scale map of your area will tell you about its topography — contours, location of open land, woods, and water — and provide clues from place names.

The garden in context
The boundary of this English garden is deliberately blurred so that it is hard to tell where the garden ends and the landscape begins. Sweeping curves and native trees in the garden provide further links with the surrounding land.

BUILDINGS IN CONTEXT

Architectural clues
Materials provide clues to soil type and local geology: this brick, tile, and flint house in Sussex, southern England, is on clay, but near chalk.

Close-up detail
Although the house is not built directly on pure chalk, it is near enough to a chalk area for flint to have been used in its construction.

LEARNING FROM THE LAND

Within the broad picture of your regional landscape there may be a range of different types of habitat, any of which may suggest inspiration for your garden, depending on your site. Refining your focus still further, look at the particular plant associations that occur in each of these specific habitats.

Downland landscape

Woodland habitat

Beech trees (Fagus sp.)

LOCAL INSPIRATION

Evolving a style for your garden calls for a design that complements not only the land itself but also the local architecture, traditions, and culture. Local distinctiveness – the characteristics of your particular area – can be a great source of inspiration. Get a feel for this by walking around your area and noting typical planting associations and landscape features, in addition to traditional materials and vernacular styles. The latter will tell you of the locally accessible materials and past construction methods and patterns. Look at walls, fences, and gates, too – anything that can provide clues. Notice scale and proportion, including how these relate to nearby features. All these factors will help integrate the garden into its place. If you live in an intensively farmed or built-up area where much of the indigenous wildlife has disappeared, the local library may be able to provide you with information about the native flora and fauna, as well as literature on the history of the people and the place. Look out, too, for local names for roads, houses, plants, even fields and crops – they may tell you a lot about your neighborhood.

Provençal stone, *right*
The soft colors of these roughly cut stone bricks from Provence in France are indicative of the colors of the earth that overlaid the uncut stone.

Vineyards, *right*
The geometric designs of early European gardens may well have been inspired by the formalized cultivated Mediterranean landscape.

Prairie vista, *left*
Low horizontal lines typify the prairie landscape in the United States.

Farm fences, *right*
Post-and-rail fences are a common sight in farmed prairie areas.

Prairie ranch house, *above*
Meadow reminiscent of wild prairie fronts a typical farmhouse.

Roof tiles, *right*
Terra-cotta roof tiles represent a long craft tradition in many Mediterranean areas.

Mediterranean style, *above*
Local materials give this southern French home its regional feel.

INTEGRATING THE LANDSCAPE

Borrowing a type or pattern of landscape from outside the garden will not only enlarge the apparent size of your plot but also link it to its terrain – an essential part of creating a natural garden. In exposed sites, or where the outlook is marred by an eyesore, a framed view may be more successful than a panoramic one; it may mean siting a tree to mask part of the view or to mirror the form of another tree beyond. This kind of echo also helps to create a transition between the domestic scale of a garden and the much larger scale of the landscape. Look at the views from upstairs windows as well as from ground level; you may discover attractions that can be opened up to a lower viewpoint by removing part of a boundary. If so, check the direction of the prevailing wind, because you may need to provide some sort of screen or planting to filter it.

An atmosphere of the veldt, *above Patrick Watson has brought the dried-up, blanched-out aridity of the African veldt into the confines of this suburban Johannesburg garden.*

Echoing a water course, *left The chatter of natural water through boulders and fieldstone is implied in this Connecticut garden designed by Janis Hall.*

Stone echoes, *above*
The natural rock outcrops of this
Argentinian pampas garden
provide a recurring theme in the
overall design by John Brookes.

Relating to the desert, *left*
Here modern Western living is
cleverly integrated by Philip
Van Wyck into one of the most
extreme and complicated natural
habitats in the world, the Sonoran
Desert, Arizona.

Reflections of nature, *above*
The water line of this swimming
pool in a Long Island garden
by Wolfgang Oehme and James
van Sweden repeats the broad
horizontal sweep of the natural
water beyond.

Basic Design Considerations

While you might know the "feel" that you want to achieve in your garden, the actual nuts and bolts of achieving this demand planning. This is essentially a two-stage process. First, you need to make an accurate survey of your plot. The site analysis should include every aspect, from orientation, existing vegetation, soil and weather conditions to wildlife features. The second stage is to decide what your own requirements are. These might include opening up views, space for sitting and entertaining, access and storage, where to put compost bins, whether you want a kitchen garden, flowers for cutting, and so on. Eventually, all these elements should blend harmoniously into their surroundings.

Evolution of a Plan

The original analysis of the property opposite is shown in the box below. For the second stage, I took a piece of tracing paper and laid it over the existing plan. I then amended the layout of the garden, taking in the owners' wishes, while at the same time drawing out its natural features. There are two major changes. First, I particularly wanted to make a feature of the stream by opening it out to create a pond. Second, I put in a new access drive from the side lane – the existing entrance to the street had become a danger spot due to increased traffic.

The Site

When making a survey of your site – here a traditional property in the north of England – first take fairly accurate measurements and sketch the outline of the area on graph paper. Mark the entrances and exits, and all other relevant features of the garden, such as:

- The relationship of your house to the garden
- The topography of your ground (i.e. changes of level)
- Any drainage patterns
- Any damp areas
- Tree and shrub positions, plus the life cycles of major plants
- Patterns of light and shade from trees or buildings on your site
- The direction of any prevailing winds
- Orientation of the sun
- Any wildlife patterns that you recognize, such as animal runs.

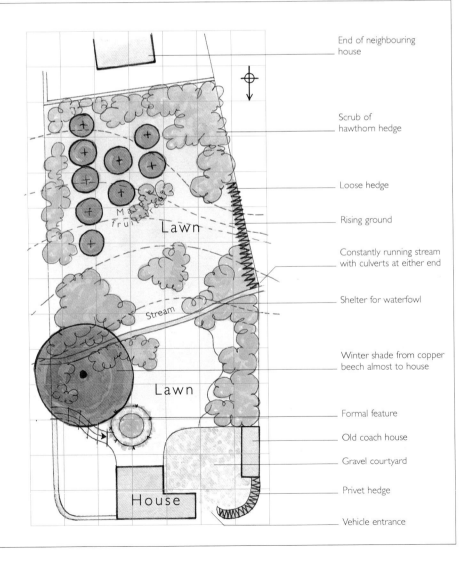

End of neighbouring house

Scrub of hawthorn hedge

Loose hedge

Rising ground

Constantly running stream with culverts at either end

Shelter for waterfowl

Winter shade from copper beech almost to house

Formal feature

Old coach house

Gravel courtyard

Privet hedge

Vehicle entrance

Main fruit area

Lawn

Lawn

Stream

House

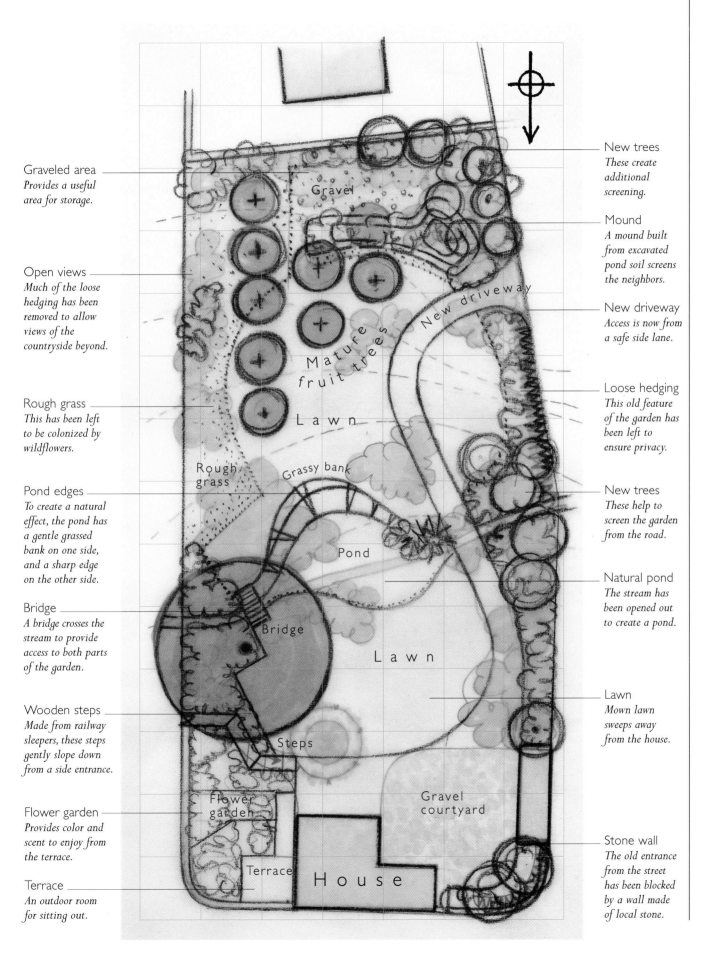

Graveled area
Provides a useful area for storage.

Open views
Much of the loose hedging has been removed to allow views of the countryside beyond.

Rough grass
This has been left to be colonized by wildflowers.

Pond edges
To create a natural effect, the pond has a gentle grassed bank on one side, and a sharp edge on the other side.

Bridge
A bridge crosses the stream to provide access to both parts of the garden.

Wooden steps
Made from railway sleepers, these steps gently slope down from a side entrance.

Flower garden
Provides color and scent to enjoy from the terrace.

Terrace
An outdoor room for sitting out.

New trees
These create additional screening.

Mound
A mound built from excavated pond soil screens the neighbors.

New driveway
Access is now from a safe side lane.

Loose hedging
This old feature of the garden has been left to ensure privacy.

New trees
These help to screen the garden from the road.

Natural pond
The stream has been opened out to create a pond.

Lawn
Mown lawn sweeps away from the house.

Stone wall
The old entrance from the street has been blocked by a wall made of local stone.

Gravel

Mature fruit trees

New driveway

Lawn

Rough grass

Grassy bank

Pond

Bridge

L a w n

Steps

Flower garden

Gravel courtyard

Terrace

H o u s e

THE FINISHED PICTURE

This Sussex garden in England demonstrates all the aspects of designing a natural garden that have been discussed in the preceding pages. Over the years, I have made suggestions to the owners about opening up the garden to the amazing view that it has on either side to a great sweep of the South Downs. The original garden plan did not take the view into account, and the detail it contained was always dwarfed by the landscape rather than including and complementing it. Near to the house the garden is at its most formal, with a brick terrace leading from the conservatory to a little pavilion that gives a vantage point from which to enjoy the incredible south-facing view. The pavilion is surrounded by decorative shrubs and perennials that do not clutter the view, and a planting of species that provide flowers throughout spring and summer also brings berries and colorful foliage in autumn. The middle distance forms a transitional area to the wildness beyond, with the pond (created by damming a stream) acting as a watery ha-ha that keeps out deer and rabbits but provides a habitat for nesting waterfowl. Throughout winter, a sward of cattails (*Typha* species) gives a decorative, yet naturalistic, appearance to the pond.

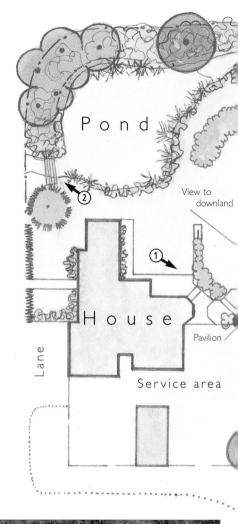

Pond

View to downland

House

Lane

Pavilion

Service area

The pavilion ①
Steps lead from a conservatory to a small pavilion, which provides a panoramic view of the South Downs beyond the garden.

Exotic planting ②
Tucked into the existing natural vegetation, exotics — in this case Gunnera manicata — introduce variety of form into the planting.

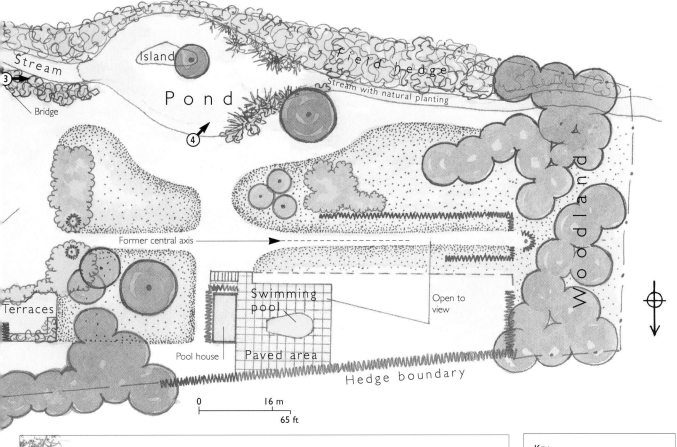

Stream

Island

P o n d

Bridge

Field hedge

Stream with natural planting

Woodland

Former central axis

Open to view

Terraces

Pool house

Swimming pool

Paved area

Hedge boundary

0   16 m
    65 ft

Opening up the views ③
The removal of the hedges that once divided the garden into rooms has created long views diagonally across the garden.

The wider landscape ④
Beyond the pool and a cultivated field, an impressive sweep of grassy downland rises up to form a green backdrop to the garden.

ELEMENTS OF DESIGN

THE PRIME OBJECTIVE in natural gardening is to integrate the garden into its setting by any means possible. This is obviously more difficult to do if you live in a terraced house in an urban location, but you can still achieve a harmonious marrying of both hard landscape and vegetation by taking note of the style and materials used in building construction and boundaries, as well as the surrounding plants, natural and cultivated. While planting will be the main feature that defines the character of your garden, boundaries, changes of level, pergolas, paving, and even furniture can add strong elements to your design. A water feature is almost essential if you wish to encourage a diversity of wildlife, and this can range from a small pool, if that is all that the scale of your garden allows, to a larger expanse of water bordered by a boggy area in which to grow marginal plants. Even a traditional swimming pool can be mellowed by the use of a soft internal color and by sympathetic design of its surroundings and accompanying structures.

Plants for definition, *right*
To prevent naturally planted areas from degenerating into a messy mass of plant material, include some strong plant forms such as this Eryngium giganteum.

An integrated design, *right*
Modern structures contrast well with a soft overlay of plants in this city garden by Bonita Bulaitis in London. The looser the planting, the stronger the design should be.

Water in the city, *left*
This brimming pool is a good blend of urban and natural elements. The inclusion of a rock demonstrates how a water feature can also be sculptural.

BOUNDARIES

The boundary impinges strongly on the look of the garden. In a rural situation, take your lead from the vernacular. Local lumber yards and agricultural shows can yield ideas for boundary enclosures and gates, or, in some areas, it may be that windbreaks and ditches are more appropriate. Real boundary problems occur as countryside merges into the city. In this situation the boundary may need to be an architectural solution, such as "arms" reaching out from the house to anchor it into the site in the form of walling. Depending on the size of the plot, you may be able to modify the boundary line if you find it unsympathetic. Planting can be used to do this, or a line between an area of rough grass and smooth. Introducing internal boundaries, perhaps in the form of hedges or groups of shrubs, can help break up your garden. In a small site, you might emphasize a diagonal line, rather than a straight line at right angles to the house, in order to give the area breadth. Remember that you do not have to use the same type of boundary all the way around the site – you can break the pattern.

Cottage-style fencing, *above*
This scrapwood fence is combined with living material.

Blending with the desert, *right*
A garden boundary made of desert stones in Arizona skillfully makes the transition from the natural to the vernacular.

Traditional dry-stone wall
This stone wall in a New England garden designed by Janis Hall is given an update in the form of cantilevered seating built into the structure.

Western-style structure
Materials found locally have been used to create a striking rustic boundary here, in a dryland setting in Arizona.

Wooden fencing
Sawn logs provide a natural boundary in temperate wetland. The logs may be woven together or set into concrete below ground level.

A living carpet
A neglected dry stone wall in England's West Country has been mellowed by the wealth of mosses and ferns growing on its shady side.

CHANGING LEVELS

Gradations of level within a garden need not be monumental – indeed, it is arguable that within a natural garden the look should be subtle. However, there are situations that call for structure in the form of steps and retaining walls, and these need to be in harmony with their surroundings. In some regions of the world, terracing that hugs the contours of the land is part of the agricultural pattern of the area, and this can be echoed in the garden. The rice fields of the East and the olive groves of Mediterranean regions are notable examples. Contoured shaping can create a wonderful flow to the garden. The prime exponent of contouring, raising the technique to an art form, is the American landscape architect Arthur Edwin Bye. He and his partner Janis Hall have created gardens that appear to have been formed by the elemental forces of nature. On a less ambitious scale, you could have fun with the soil from the excavation of a swimming pool; even if you dig down only a little, you can create mounds on either side of a sunken area. In general, the forms you make are likely to be fairly gentle to simulate natural contours, but if you have an outlook onto craggy peaks and steep hills, you might use stronger land forms to create a more integrated effect.

Steps in scale with the surroundings
In this California garden by Isabelle Greene, railroad ties create sympathetic steps.

Changing levels with decking
Decking and stairs wind their way down this subtropical garden in New Zealand.

Contouring the landscape, *right*
In this Connecticut garden, landscape architect Janis Hall has created rippling hillocks, echoing the movement of water. The changing light during the course of the day continually alters the effect.

A terraced feature, *left*
The traditional walled terraces of an olive grove have become part of the design of this stepped garden in Provence in the south of France.

ALTERNATIVE SURFACES

A smooth expanse of lawn is often considered essential to a garden, yet our love affair with grass is not practical; we feed and water, spike and rake only to crewcut the resulting healthy growth. Global warming and drought, sympathetic substitutes, and just plain shortage of time have made alternatives to the lawn attractive – particularly where space is limited. A graveled and planted surface can look very effective, while an area of paving can contain other materials to break it up and add interest. For example, you could use weathered concrete slabs, which resemble natural stone, and work a brick pattern through them. If you want some grass that will require less work than a manicured lawn, lay your slabs some distance apart and grow grass between them – you can still mow over the surface. If hard surfaces are not to your taste, consider a heather, sedge, thyme, or chamomile lawn, moss, or even plain brushed earth or sand. These treatments are, of course, not applicable everywhere, and much will depend upon climate and usage. An area of grass lawn can still be desirable, but the scale can be reduced where other treatments are an option.

Woodland groundcover

In this Massachusetts garden there is a natural groundcover of the plants that thrive in light deciduous woodland, with a preponderance of Phlox × procumbens. *Dense carpets of narrow, dark green leaves are smothered in spring with sprays of rich lilac-pink flowers.*

Softening hard surfaces

Random paving has rivulets of Mazus reptans *'Albus' planted between the joints. Grasses or thymes might provide alternative plantings.*

Forest floor, *above*
*A tapestry of cushion
moss covers a woodland
floor in Britain, with
fairly dense shade
above. Beyond, native
sedges catch the light.*

Rock garden, *right*
*Pebbles and boulders
emphasize the gritty
overall surface of this
Arizona garden, while
also acting as an
effective mulch.*

WATER

Most natural gardeners recognize the importance of water in the garden to provide a wide range of wildlife and plant habitats. A wild look may be the aim, but it must be kept under control, since wet conditions can foster rampant growth. I think that the first criterion should be scale. Have as much water as possible – the larger the area, the easier a pond is to manage – but make sure it looks natural, too, and in proportion to the site. We all know that water runs downhill, so site water at the lowest point of your layout. You can fudge the issue with ground shaping, but make sure that your solution is convincing. Small pools are tricky and can become overgrown in a single season. Their small scale is often compounded by a tendency to include little features around them. Resist this temptation at all costs.

Water splash
Landscape architect Patrick Watson has continued water across the driveway to provide a decorative water splash in this South African city garden.

Desert oasis, *above*
Still water in the desert is rare; here, the skillful combination of rock and native plants has made a convincing association.

Pool in a city garden, *right*
A rock edging and generous subtropical planting make this pool in a city garden in New Zealand appear part of a natural landscape.

Still waters

This natural pool in southwest England displays the layers of vegetation that provide a range of different habitats for wildlife.

Moving water

In a mountainous area such as this one in Ireland, rocks and moving water can provide the example to follow in a garden setting.

Artificial wetland

One of the earliest examples of created wetland, intended as both a decorative and an educational feature, is found at the Thijsse Park in Amsterdam, the Netherlands.

FURNITURE

Garden furniture design has moved on considerably from the days when the demand was for formal pieces that referred back to an earlier, halcyon period of grand living. Many new designers are crossing the divide between practical items for the garden and something more naturalistic and sculptural. Their pieces are distinguished by their highly individualistic style, often combining found materials with a thoroughly modern approach. The value of such work, I believe, goes beyond it being both idiosyncratically beautiful and useful — by example, it encourages us to explore our own creative resources and to find our own way of connecting with the environment in which we live.

Maritime links, *above*
A container made from iron chain makes an ideal plant holder for a seaside garden.

Rustic design, *above*
This simple wooden seat provides a perfect place to rest a while on a woodland wander.

Multipurpose seating, *right*
A stone slab that doubles as both seat and table combines usefulness with a natural look.

Sitting four square, *left*
Made of found wood from the farmyard, this really chunky bench seat has the simplicity of Adirondack furniture.

Spiraling bench, *above*
A carved wooden picnic bench by Alison Crowther takes natural furniture into a new dimension with its sculptural, organic qualities.

LAND ART

While we increasingly exploit the Earth's mineral resources, we no longer use its potential visual wealth to the fullest. The march of urbanization and technological sophistication seems to have cost us our sense of being rooted in the land. In the past, and still in many so-called primitive societies, people have drawn inspiration from nature to create objects that were both of and for the land, often with a mystical significance; think of stone circles, figures cut into chalk hillsides, Aboriginal sand paintings, Native American carvings. Some were linked to festivals or folklore, especially in relation to the natural cycles of the seasons. Others were a celebration of people's relationship with the land.

We could make greater use of our creative resources and re-establish that connection to our environment. There could be a return to that deeper understanding. Many artists are now working in natural materials, using found objects, and exploring the rich palette of textures and forms suggested by the natural world and their own local surroundings. You might even decide to create your own piece of land art, inspired by your site and locale.

Flint sculpture, *above*
This piece by Ivan Hicks is made of found flints and is set against the background of a flint wall.

Willow sculpture, *above*
*Willow (*Salix *spp.) grows in damp places, and here it has been shaped by Sophie Ryder to create a herd of deer entering a natural pool in the Forest of Dean in England.*

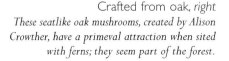

Crafted from oak, *right*
These seatlike oak mushrooms, created by Alison Crowther, have a primeval attraction when sited with ferns; they seem part of the forest.

Bridge, center
Paul Cooper's "Two Circles in a Stone Bridge" is built in an abandoned quarry. The sculpture has a western exposure to catch the setting sun.

Stone vase, left
Joe Smith creates garden urns, building up their curvy shapes with slivers of local limestone.

NATURAL PLANTING

O nce you have decided what you want to achieve in your
garden, and built the bones of it, you can think about the
planting. This is the part most people long to plunge into, often at
the expense of the initial planning – but I believe that the more
natural the approach, the stronger the basic design needs to be.
The more established your starting point – mature trees, aged
structures – the more natural the result will be. When adapting an
existing garden, you need to work with an understanding of what
would emerge if you allowed natural layers of vegetation to take
over from annual and perennial weeds. It is this organic evolution
of a habitat that you seek to develop, while keeping in tune with
the site so that your garden will not ultimately require detailed
maintenance. Take heart from the fact that the worse your site, in
terms of old horticultural practice – waterlogged, stony, shaded
by trees – the better it probably is in terms of the natural
approach. Don't rush to eradicate all weeds, as by doing so you
will destroy established plant and wildlife associations. While some
native plants really are too invasive for a small space, others may
be incorporated into a more general planting done the natural way.

A natural combination, *above*
Grasses and sedges will fit harmoniously with
a general planting plan.

Wetland plant association, *right*
The garden of Dutch artist Ton ter Linden
includes this attractive waterside planting.

PLANTING ASSOCIATIONS

The planting in your garden should depend not just on which plants you select but also on how they grow. Observe planting associations in different habitats – woodland, wetland, grassland, and so on – and then adapt them to your own garden. This approach moves away from the conventional herbaceous-border style of planting in clumps of three, five, and seven; instead, we drift plants in a less defined and rigid medium than the border.

Few plants naturally stay in neat little clumps – after all, they reproduce by spreading themselves in all sorts of ways. So the natural garden is looser and more sprawling than the conventional one – like the drift and flow effect of nature – and this is its charm. You do not have to be too purist and stick entirely with indigenous species; you can adjust and adapt. But keep in mind what you know of planting design. You need one or two "specials", or dominant plants, and a strong, preferably evergreen, skeleton, with decorative shrubs and perennials. Drift annuals and bulbs as infill material through later-blooming perennials. The idea is to temper the natural way with a practical approach, and the result will look wonderfully different from more conventional groupings.

FIELD STUDY SAMPLE

To understand drift and flow, observe it in nature. Sketch a plan view of a natural plant grouping. Identify the habitat to learn about plant associations in relation to growing conditions. Capture plant groups with a camera and use them as a reference when planning your planting.

Natural flowering meadow

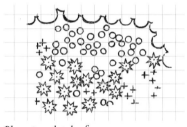

Plan view sketch of area

HOW PLANT GROUPING HAS CHANGED

Gertrude Jekyll
Gertrude Jekyll was one of the first gardeners to move away from the formal bedding designs of the 19th century. Influenced by natural associations and cottage style, she introduced freer groupings with an emphasis on shape and texture (below).

Modernist approach
Jekyll's interest in form and shape was taken up by designers of the Modernist school and later. They planted in stronger blocks of plant material with a greater emphasis on plant forms than on flower color, often using exotic plants (below).

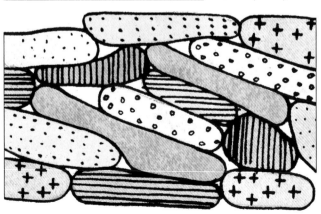

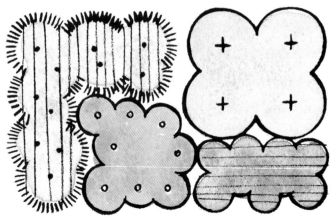

Planting a wetland habitat
In my own garden, I am attempting a wetland association of plants. Where the soil is drier, decorative viburnums grow with the rampant Heracleum sphondylium (cow parsnip, or hogweed) and Ligularia spp.

New romantics
Looser perennial groupings began to replace architectural-style massings. This was a softer, romantic look, less based on exotic species. The line between cultivated bed and lawn was often blurred with the use of hard materials (below).

Natural style
The influence of natural habitat associations in garden planting is now clear. Drifted material, largely of noninvasive natives, is more random and meadow-like, but repetition is important if the effect is not to look staccato (below).

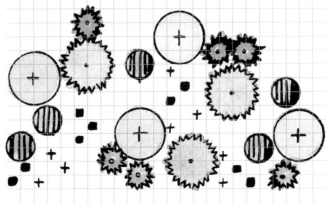

CONDITIONING THE GROUND

Many native plants prefer an impoverished soil, and the closer to their natural habitat they are in the garden, the better. So a poor soil is often more conducive to natural gardening than one that has been artificially enriched; a new site may provide an excellent base. However, bare soil loses water rapidly and encourages colonizing weeds. Covering the surface with a mulch reduces evaporation from the surface, thus maximizing the moisture-holding content of your soil. It also prevents unwanted weeds from gaining a foothold and helps to regulate soil temperature. In nature, vegetation acts as a mulch by clothing the earth; as it dies back, it forms a nutrient-rich layer upon the surface. Eventually, this mulch decomposes into the topsoil and conditions it. The natural gardener mimics this natural process by adding a mulch. The type of mulch you use will vary according to your area and conditions. Composted household waste is ideal, as is any locally available organic matter such as seaweed, bark chips, sawdust, cocoa shells, spent mushroom compost, or manure.

Heather and gorse moorland
Groundcover acts as a living blanket over the earth; as plants die, they decompose into a mulch that helps to improve the poor, acidic soil.

Natural mulch, *above*
Worms and micro-organisms take down dead matter on the earth's surface and break this up, conditioning the soil.

Shady forest floor, *left*
Fallen leaves form a natural mulch under a dense woodland canopy, where little else can grow.

GARDEN MULCHES

On exposed ground, mulching the soil reduces moisture loss, helps suppress weeds (which also use up water), conditions the soil, and protects it from erosion by wind and rain.

Animal manure
Horse and chicken manure make good mulch and are nutrient-rich.

Grass clippings
These should be about 6in (15cm) deep; apply after drying slightly.

Cocoa shell
The shells of cocoa beans last well, and add nutrients to the soil.

Bark chips
Bark is an expensive mulch, but will last for at least three years.

NATURAL GARDENING

This section contains specific regional case histories, showing how natural gardeners in various parts of the world have formed partnerships with their particular locations. Here are living examples of what I believe is the way ahead – to work in harmony with nature in our gardens, not against it. To this end, I have also included many practical techniques and advice on natural gardening.

COASTAL

TEMPERATE

WOODLAND

WETLAND

GRASSLAND

DRYLAND

MEDITERRANEAN

TROPICAL

CITY

COASTAL GARDENS

S A NEW GARDENER by the ocean, you might think that coastal habitats fall into two obvious categories: a sandy beach with dunes behind it, or, at the other extreme, rocks and pebbles. In fact, there are dozens of variations between these broad types, from flat estuaries and salt marshes to clifftop locations rich in maritime grasses and other flora. Differing climates – whether Mediterranean, tropical, or temperate – introduce additional permutations. Even so, the coastal garden has well-defined parameters within which the gardener must work. Exposure to sea spray and strong, salt-laden winds are the greatest hazards; the compensations are milder temperatures and a unique range of plants. Ocean views are another bonus, and it is often possible to integrate the maritime panorama into the garden layout.

Coastal groundcover
Swaths of Malephora crocea *play an important role in stabilizing this California beach* (above). *This carpeting effect can be copied in a garden context* (right), *here using* Limonium *and* Pelargonium *species.*

THE SEASIDE GARDENER

Many gardeners find a coastal location daunting, particularly when trying to maintain a traditional garden filled with exotic and tender plants, most of them unsuited to the special conditions. There is another way: allow the salty winds to govern plant choice and layout, and choose plants that have adapted to this demanding environment. Observe those native subjects that grow at sea level, along cliff paths or in rocky crevices, and consider how you might interpret these in a garden context. Salt-tolerant trees and shrubs can be grown as protective screening at the garden perimeter, but where the outlook is good, consider a partial shelter belt to make the most of the view. And to link the garden with the shore beyond, use materials that characterize the coastline, such as rocks, pebbles or shale, sand, and shells.

Open beach, *left*
A bleak, windswept pebble beach in Kent, England, is the location for a nuclear power station; it is also where the late filmmaker Derek Jarman chose to live and where he created his celebrated garden.

Found objects, *below*
Jarman used a range of native seaside species to create a garden that expressed a very personal sense of place. Flotsam found along the shore was turned into land art to complement the planting.

Shelter from the wind, *above*
Along a beach in New South Wales, Australia,
clusters of pine trees filter the force of the wind.

Coastal bush planting, *left*
This house nestles in native Australian bush
vegetation of eucalyptus and Acacia baileyana.

GENERAL CONDITIONS

A stretch of Cape shoreline, South Africa

CLIMATE

TEMPERATURES: In coastal regions, conditions
are milder than they are inland, with both
hot and cold extremes of temperature
moderated by the mass of the sea.

WIND: Exposure to drying and salt-laden
winds some distance from the shore is a
major factor affecting garden layout,
perimeter screening, and plant choice.

SOIL

The soil pH varies, depending on the
area and underlying bedrock – on chalky
cliffs the overlying soil will be alkaline,
while on craggy granite coastlines it will
tend to be acid. Soil may be sandy, rocky,
or pebbly, but is typically low in organic
matter, and high in salt.

TERRAIN

Coastal habitats vary widely, with the
terrain ranging from steep rocky slopes
and chalky clifftops to mud flats, estuaries,
and sandy beaches, which may include
dunes or be edged with native trees.

OPEN TO THE ELEMENTS

SET AGAINST THE backdrop of Table Mountain, South Africa, this house and its stunning garden sit high above a rocky beach. Designed by landscape architect Patrick Watson, the garden demonstrates a brilliant molding with its setting. The most striking feature is the pool area with its arrangement of local granite boulders – when viewed from the house it flows seamlessly into the ocean beyond. At the front of the house, rocky banks on either side of the entrance steps receive a soft spray to re-create the misty habitat of rare *Disa* orchids that grow in the mountain gorges behind. Mixed with ferns and mosses, these delicate natives are now starting to carpet their new home, truly blending this garden into its coastal site.

View across the pool ①
Looking away from the sea, the view includes the steep hillside and strong rock forms of the National Park beyond.

Water feature ②
The steps are flanked by water-chute balustrades lined with stones and ending in molded basins. Next to these, rocky banks are filled with orchids, ferns, and mosses.

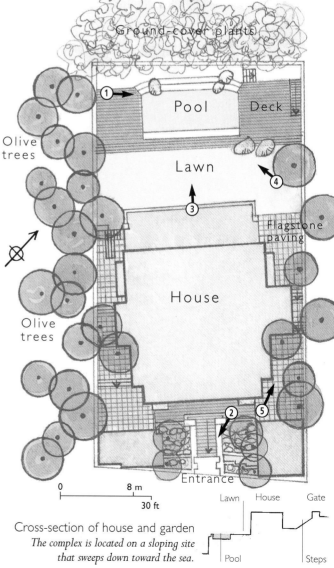

Ground-cover plants

Pool

Deck

Olive trees

Lawn

Olive trees

Flagstone paving

House

Entrance

0   8 m
30 ft

Cross-section of house and garden
The complex is located on a sloping site that sweeps down toward the sea.

Lawn | House | Gate
Pool | Steps

Bold lines ③
The craggy forms of Cape granite boulders at the edge of the deck echo the beach below and visually link the blue, blue sea with the swimming pool at house level. Between the pool deck and the house is a lawn of Cynodon transvaalensis *on which to sunbathe.*

Fusion with nature, *left* ④
The pool, cut into the line of the headland, seems to float above the Indian Ocean.

A seat in the shade, *below* ⑤
Native olive trees shade a garden seat in a small, sheltered side courtyard. The paving is terracotta slabs with grassy joints.

GARDEN PROFILE

ORIGINS

LOCATION: The garden lies 115ft (35m) above a rocky beach near Cape Town, South Africa.
AREA: Approximately 1⅓ acres (0.5 hectare).
HISTORY: Previously, the garden was filled with exotic plants; it was redesigned in 1993.

Regal Pelargonium *thrives on the coast.*

SITE CHARACTERISTICS

SOIL TYPE: The soil is largely clay, with a thin, gritty upper layer. The bedrock is granite.
CLIMATE: Coastal Mediterranean in character. Pulverizing winds are a major factor.
ORIENTATION: The garden faces west.

SELECTED PLANT LIST

Adiantum spp., *Albuca nelsonii, Amaryllis belladonna, Aristea major, Asplenium lobatum, Babiana* spp., *Blechnum* spp., *Cyclopia sessiliflora, Cyrtanthus* spp., *Dierama pendulum, Disa uniflora, Eucomis autumnalis, Ficus pumila, Gladiolus alatus, Hermannia saccifera, Hypoxis setosa, Moraea aristata, Nerine sarniensis, Olea africana, Oxalis* spp., *Phygelius aequalis, Rhus crenata, Schizostylis coccinea.*

A COASTAL DESIGN

LET YOUR IMAGINATION roam freely over the elements of the natural landscape you live in. At the center of these pages is an artist's impression of a garden design I have drawn up inspired by a coastal location. (A thematic scheme is repeated in each chapter throughout this section.) This garden, below a summer beach home, could be almost anywhere. It is approached down sand-blown wooden steps that open out to provide a picnic deck. The garden is contained by low gabion walls (see p.67) that provide shelter on blustery days. Similar structures are used to retain high banks on the sides of highways, but these are a smaller, domestic version. The gabions are galvanized metal frames, filled with local stones and built up to form a wall, which soon becomes a screen against the wind. Within the garden space, there are big masses of groundcover planting – mainly succulents – that can withstand both the blistering wind and the drought. The swaths of colorful groundcover drift into the seaside plantings behind the sheltering gabion.

CULTURAL INFLUENCES

The forces of wind and sea in a coastal setting weather artificial objects very quickly and mellow them. To counteract this, the idiom is to use bright color for painted surfaces. Decking, boardwalks, and pontoons provide inspiration for a range of garden structures, as do coastal protection devices such as beach groins and gabions.

Beach groins, low tide

Harbor protection

Brightly colored wooden boats

Treasures on the beach

A JOHN BROOKES PLAN

This simple layout attempts to re-create one of those hot, still places you sometimes find among sand dunes, with mesembryanthemums providing a bright carpet of flowers within the garden.

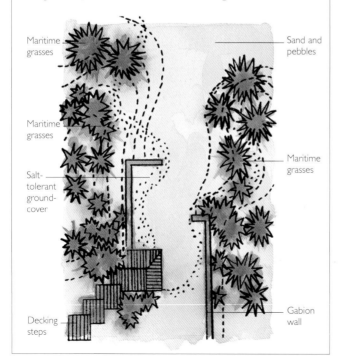

Maritime grasses

Maritime grasses

Salt-tolerant groundcover

Decking steps

Sand and pebbles

Maritime grasses

Gabion wall

NATURAL INSPIRATIONS

This garden conjures up a coastal
location of warm pockets of shelter
within sand dunes, of gritty sand
underfoot, and the reedy smell of
marram grass baked in summer heat.
Observe the range of habitats and
plant associations found in such a
setting, and how they change the
farther back you go inland.

*Shells come in
various shapes
and colors*

*Some hardy plants will
grow on rocks*

*Natural
patterns, such
as sand "waves"
on a beach, may
be a source of
design ideas*

CREATING A COASTAL AMBIENCE

A COASTAL GARDEN is one of the most difficult to design and establish. The scale of the sea itself will always dominate, and then there is the wind, which is salt-laden at that. A sheltering screen is vital; it helps to stabilize an often sandy habitat and reduces erosion and moisture loss. Coarse gravel is more stable than sand but contains few nutrients, so should be conditioned with the incorporation of organic matter. To improve the conditions, screens may be planted or constructed of brushwood, or sturdier structures such as gabions or driftwood groins may be built. The shelter they provide enables an association of salt-tolerant plants to be established.

NATURAL INSPIRATION

In southern California, landscape architect Isabelle Greene took the line and pattern of the waves washing upon the shore and turned them into a design for a broad wooden deck that overlooks the ocean view, with curving steps leading down to the beach. Note that the steps are not all the same width, repeating the irregularity of the receding surf, and are ideal as landings on which to sit or sunbathe. They successfully combine a strong graphic quality with naturalistic forms.

Ocean influence
The linear pattern of the gentle waves lapping onto the seashore was the designer's inspiration when creating a garden in this coastal site in southern California.

Curved decking terrace
The wide, shallow steps help to link the house and garden with their natural surroundings as well as forming a useful extension to the terrace by offering extra seating space.

BOARDWALKS

In seaside gardens, boardwalks made of pressure-treated wood can be used to provide a secure footing and protect the ground from disturbance. They can also be used to cross sand dunes. Lighter, portable walkways, known as duckboards, are useful for temporary access. In most areas, any construction on dunes must follow local or federal conservation regulations.

Boardwalk path
This boardwalk path forms an approach to the house and is entirely in keeping with its surroundings. Grasses planted to stabilize the sand will soon knit together to establish an exciting visual contrast of artificial and natural forms.

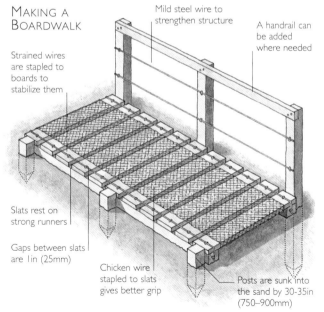

MAKING A BOARDWALK

Mild steel wire to strengthen structure

A handrail can be added where needed

Strained wires are stapled to boards to stabilize them

Slats rest on strong runners

Gaps between slats are 1in (25mm)

Chicken wire stapled to slats gives better grip

Posts are sunk into the sand by 30-35in (750–900mm)

Construction of a boardwalk
A permanent raised boardwalk, accessed by a wooden ramp or steps, protects an unstable or drifting surface such as sand dunes. For surer footing, you can add a handrail, and lay chicken wire over the slats.

MAKING GABIONS

In pebble or gravel areas, a tough structural windbreak, such as a wall made from wire-mesh gabions, looks appropriate. Rigid wire panels are used for box-type gabions and chain-link fencing for tubular ones. The spaces between the stones trap sand or gravel, and plant life starts to establish a living wall.

A gabion wall
Place the gabions so that they take the brunt of the wind. You may want to work organic matter into the gaps between the stones to encourage plants to establish themselves in the wall more quickly.

1 The flat gabion frame
Lay the preformed wire frame flat in the area where you want to use the gabion, as they are heavy to move once filled.

2 Putting it together
Fold the wire frame into a box, securing it firmly with galvanized metal rings. For extra strength, cross brace it as you fill it.

3 Filling and closing up
Place the frame in position, then fill it with large stones so that they are fairly tightly packed together. Secure the lid with wire.

4 Starting a small wall
Use the gabions like giant bricks to form a retaining wall or wind shelter in which plants can become established over time.

BRUSHWOOD SCREENS

If you are creating a tall shelter from the wind, it should not be a solid barrier but a filtering screen that lets the wind flow over and through it while reducing its force. One way to create a fence is to use dense bundles of brushwood (see below). A stronger version can be made by securing the bundles between parallel strained wires or crossbars – even in an established fence.

Sink the brushwood deeply into a hole or trench.

The bundles are set into a mortar mix.

Making a brushwood screen
Lash together pieces of brushwood into bundles. Plunge each bundle into a hole, and then backfill with a mortar mix. The mortar will set hard and withstand a battering from wind.

A brushwood screen made with supports
In this coastal site, brushwood has been woven between the strained wires and sturdy wooden verticals of an established fence to create a screen that filters the wind and harmonizes with the landscape.

TEMPERATE GARDENS

MANY PARTS OF EUROPE and the eastern United States enjoy a temperate climate, with comparatively mild temperatures and no harsh extremes. Most of the broadleaved woodland that once covered these lands has been cleared and cultivated to create arable land, hay meadows, rolling hills, and lush pastures for grazing. Some parts are still bounded by woodland edges, a haven for wildlife, but many such habitats have been destroyed by intensive farming methods. The gardener can do much to stem the tide of this rural decline by planting native species – many of which are the original forms of hybridized garden plants in any case – in order to encourage wildlife. The size of the garden isn't important: from acorns come oak trees, and even small efforts can produce spectacular results.

A harmonious grouping
This stunning garden in the Netherlands (right) created by Ton ter Linden picks up on the lush pastures of the surrounding habitat (above), skillfully blending suitable garden plants with native wetland species.

THE RURAL GARDENER

Increasingly, I believe that there are two positive ways in which the temperate garden can develop: either as a productive cottage garden, or as an entirely decorative but wilder type of garden. Pristine lawns and highly cultivated borders are replaced by looser, airier plantings, selected to suit a particular habitat. Following rural traditions, there may also be scented shrub roses, fruit trees, and a variety of herbs, depending on the area. Annuals and biennials are left to self-seed and create a managed yet glorious disarray. Indigenous plants, adapted to the local conditions, are allowed to thrive – although monitored – bringing insect life into the garden, and in turn attracting other wildlife. Instead of maintaining the garden, you will be *managing* it, which I believe will mark a true change of direction.

Link with the landscape, *left*
A wilder type of garden in Sussex, England, which blends seamlessly with its pastoral setting.

Downs and fields, *above*
High pasture has long been grazed by sheep, with the flatter areas used for arable farming.

Soft boundary, *above*
Cultivated plants give way to clover lawn, then Osteospermum *sp. and* Geranium sylvaticum.

Temperate meadow, *top*
*Buttercups (*Ranunculus *sp.) combine with* Camassia *sp. and red clover in a cultivated meadow.*

GENERAL CONDITIONS

CLIMATE

Temperate zones are characterized by mild temperatures, without harsh extremes, and sufficient rainfall, and so provide benign growing conditions. However, where the landmass is vast, an inland "continental" climate develops, with much hotter summers and far colder winters.

SOIL

Soil type varies according to region and terrain. On chalky downland, for example, the soil is typically thin and alkaline, whereas in a peat area it will be acid. For growing a wide range of plants, the ideal soil is a good loam, with the right balance of sand and clay and a high humus content.

Wildflowers on British pasture

TERRAIN

These regions include most types of terrain, such as woodlands, grasslands, and wetlands, all providing very different plant habitats. However, most of these areas have been cleared or drained to make way for agriculture and habitation and are therefore open lands, as here.

THE LAWS OF NATURE

"MY GARDEN SHOULD be like nature, without apparent logic," says Henk Gerritsen about Priona, his garden in Holland. "You cannot see it and you certainly cannot understand it, but you can just sense the logic." At first, only wild species were planted – not necessarily Dutch natives – where Henk thought each would grow best, to create a series of distinct gardens. This wildflower-only policy was gradually abandoned in favor of the more relaxed approach taken by the garden's cofounder, the late Anton Schlepers, who liked to see garden favorites, too. Henk feels that the garden has gained in interest as a result. He adds, "There are hardly any principles left. Principles in a garden are blown away in a storm, freeze in an unusually cold winter, or crumble in a hot, dry summer. The only principle is the total absence of chemicals. The wildlife that comes to eat my garden is welcomed. Consequently, I have never seen plagues in my garden."

Butterfly plants, right
The butterfly garden is situated in a sunny, fertile spot. Species such as Dianthus *and* Scabiosa *attract some 30 different kinds of butterfly, but the plant community is fragile and needs some guiding.*

STRUCTURE IN THE VEGETABLE GARDEN

The large vegetable garden, located close to the main house at Priona, is filled with vegetables, such as leeks, carrots, and cabbages, grown exclusively for their flowers. These vegetables are allowed to sow themselves spontaneously and are combined with other self-sown annuals and biennials such as poppies, verbascum, and *Cleome* species.

The result is a colorful profusion of vegetation that, by the end of June, is dominated by flowering parsnip (see right). In contrast to the exuberant planting, the paths in the vegetable garden are laid out in a regular, geometric fashion. These give the garden much-needed coherence and prevent it from looking like a total wilderness.

Linking forms
Seen from this angle, the line of the path in the vegetable garden reflects the roof of the house beyond.

The "pot-square," *left*
*Frost-tender perennials are kept
in pots. The softer parts of the
Onopordum sp. on the left will
be completely eaten by caterpillars
later in the year, leaving a skeleton
that will stand all winter.*

Vegetable garden, *below*
*During early summer, the
vegetable garden is filled with
the unusual and attractive heads
of flowering parsnip.*

PLAN ANALYSIS

PRIONA IS MADE up of a series of different gardens (see pp.72–73), each one established to suit a specific environment, from extremely shaded areas with poor, acid soil to sunny plots and fertile ground, with everything in between. The gardens range through naturalized woodland, a flower garden for butterflies, and a wetland area, to a large vegetable patch, a meadow garden, and a formal garden filled with yew and boxwood clipped into informal shapes. Some of the gardens are stable and require little maintenance. Others – in particular the butterfly garden, the vegetable garden, and an area known as the garden "behind the hedge" – need constant guidance.

Woodland

Garden haven for butterflies, *left* ①
A pink Geranium sp. adds a flash of color to a triangular bed.

A romantic water garden, *below* ②
According to Henk, the pond looks like "the one Ophelia drowned in, as depicted in the painting by Millais."

GARDEN PROFILE

ORIGINS

LOCATION: Schuinesloot, the Netherlands.
AREA: 5 acres (2 hectares).
HISTORY: Started in 1983 with Henk's late friend Anton Schlepers, on farmland that had belonged to Anton's family since 1860.

SITE CHARACTERISTICS

SOIL TYPE: The land is on a sandy glacial deposit, in what was once the largest bog in Europe, the Bourtanger Moor – now drained. The soil is poor but enriched near the house with nearly 150 years of domestic waste.

A bright corner of yellow violas and honeysuckle

CLIMATE: Conditions are temperate, but with continental features. The average annual rainfall is 30–32in (750–800mm).
ORIENTATION: Mainly south-facing (i.e., sunny), but there are also shaded areas.

SELECTED PLANT LIST

Achillea spp., *Cirsium heterophyllum, Clematis* spp., *Dianthus carthusianorum, Geranium nodosum, G. psilostemon, Knautia macedonica, Onopordum* spp., *Origanum vulgare, Scabiosa lucida, Sedum telephium, Silene vulgaris, Verbascum olympicum, Verbena bonariensis.*

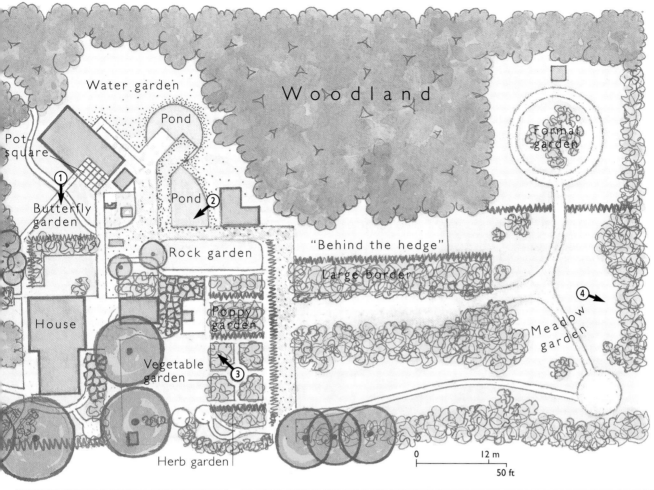

Water garden

Pond

Woodland

Pot-square

Formal garden

Butterfly garden ①

Pond ②

Rock garden

"Behind the hedge"

Large border

House

Poppy garden

Vegetable garden ③

Meadow garden ④

Herb garden

0   12 m
50 ft

Vegetable garden ③
Verbascum olympicum, *parsnip, strawberries, poppies, and purple* Atriplex *spp. (orache) create an attractive mix in front of the chicken house.*

Meadow garden ④
*Plants such as rosebay willowherb (*Epilobium *spp.), achillea, and* Cirsium heterophyllum *thrive in the meadow garden.*

A WINDSWEPT VIEW

ESTABLISHING A GARDEN in an exposed area is not without its problems, especially if, like the owners of this chalk downland garden in southern England, you wish to link the house to the sweeping landscape beyond and at the same time provide a degree of shelter. Fortunately, the garden came with a clump of mature beeches – a strong link with the past, for this area was once rich pasture for sheep, and such clusters provided shelter for lambing. Further planting was added to link the trees with the adjoining gravel garden, which is partially filled with the same flowers that once brightened the finely cropped sward. It is left open so that the land appears to roll away from the house to the horizon.

Cottage-style entrance
The front garden includes a Rosa *'Penelope' with lavender in the foreground; behind the roses is a* Paeonia lutea, *with angelica.*

Before planting, *left*
The gravel garden was positioned to take advantage of a gap in the existing hedgerow with expansive views beyond. Lawn was not considered here.

The gravel garden established, *above*
The artist in the family has thrown downland flower seeds about at random and planted many bulbs, combining the best of wild and cultivated, to provide subjects for her to paint.

GARDEN PROFILE

ORIGINS

LOCATION: Rolling chalk downland in the south of England.

HISTORY: Work on the garden started in 1984; previously, the land was roughly gardened. In addition to the main gravel garden, there is a small wild pool on one side surrounded by rushes and native yellow flag iris (*Iris pseudacorus*). There are also plantings on the north side of the house, which are mainly in shade.

AREA: The garden covers approximately ½ acre (0.2 hectare).

Blue love-in-a-mist (Nigella damascena)

SITE CHARACTERISTICS

SOIL TYPE: Light and chalky; the naturally high pH has been modified to near neutral by previous cultivation and added organic matter, which has improved the condition and water-holding capacity of the soil. The gravel in the main garden also acts as a useful water-retaining mulch.

CLIMATE: A mild temperate climate, but fairly exposed, with strong winds.

ORIENTATION: The garden encircles the house, so there is a range of exposures. The site is open and mainly in full sun.

THE GRAVEL GARDEN

The space in front of the house was originally laid out with a fairly conventional garden in mind, although it included an open gravel area bordered by perennials and lime-loving shrubs rather than a more traditional lawn. Self-seeding perennials such as species of *Alchemilla* and *Sisyrinchium* were planted direct through the gravel into the soil below to soften its stark look early on. Gradually, over a ten-year period, the style of the garden has loosened up enormously, with a variety of foliage and flowers balancing the harshness of the gravel.

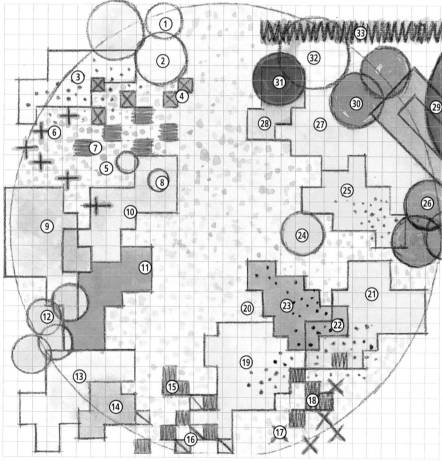

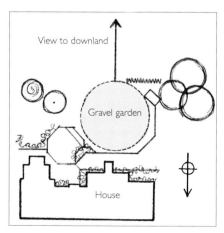

Garden layout
The gravel garden is ideally located to make the most of the south-facing exposure and an uninterrupted view of downland pastures.

KEY TO THE PLANTING PLAN

1. *Rosa* 'The Fairy'
2. *Rosa* 'Penelope'
3. *Verbascum olympicum* × 20
4. *Festuca glauca* × 5
5. *Allium aflatunense* × 25
6. *Angelica* spp. × 5
7. *Echinops ritro* × 5
8. *Paeonia lutea* × 2
9. *Digitalis* spp. × 30
10. *Aquilegia* spp. × 25
11. *Geranium* spp. × 22
12. *Potentilla fruticosa* × 4
13. *Aquilegia spp.* × 30
14. *Primula* spp. × 12
15. *Thymus caespititius* × 25
16. *Phlox procumbens* × 5
17. *Iris sibirica* × 5
18. *Thymus vulgaris* × 6
19. *Nigella* spp. × 34
20. *Allium cristophii* × 25
21. *Alchemilla mollis* × 20
22. *Allium aflatunense* × 25
23. *Geranium* spp. × 20
24. *Phlomis fruticosa*
25. *Nectaroscordum siculum*
26. *Sisyrinchium striatum* × 15
27. *Aquilegia* spp. × 25
28. *Alchemilla mollis* × 12
29. *Rosa* 'Mme. Alfred Carrière'
30. *Rosa* 'William Lobb'
31. *Rosa* 'Nuits de Young'
32. *Rosa* 'Nevada'
33. Hedge of *Crataegus* spp.

MAKING A MEADOW

HARD AS I MIGHT TRY to fight the romantic hayfield approach to meadow gardening, I cannot, for there is a timeless beauty about a meadow in full flower. At her home in the English Midlands, Miriam Rothschild echoes the poet Tennyson's passion for a "careless, ordered garden." She was dismayed some time ago to realize "that wildflowers had been drained, bulldozed, weed-killered, and fertilized out of the fields… we were now in a countryside reminiscent of a pool table, and must do something about it." You could follow her example and grow tall grasses laced with dwarf narcissus, species tulips, alliums, and irises. Add roses, both cultivated and wild, and near the house grow scented shrubs and climbers (here buddleia and clematis) that attract butterflies.

In full flower
A foaming sea of cow parsnip (Anthriscus sylvestris) surges up to a row of cottages on the estate. There are now about 120 native species, from wild garlic to bee orchids, in the lawns surrounding the house, as well as introduced species such as beargrass and martagon lilies.

Cornfield mixture
Gravel paths are lined with cornflowers, oxeye daisies, corn marigolds, poppies, and flax — a mix wryly named "Farmer's Nightmare."

Naturalized bulbs in grass, *left*
A mown path sweeps through long grass planted with daffodils and other bulbs such as alliums. These can compete with the vigor of the grass and are compatible with the wildflowers, the seeds of which were collected from nearby derelict land.

Colorful wall climbers, *right*
The mauve plumes of a mature wisteria and the pale blooms of Clematis montana *create a frame of flowers and foliage around a doorway.*

Flowering fruit trees
Above the grasses and daffodils, flowering cherries and plums provide a display of blossoms in spring and foliage color in autumn.

Grassy path, *left*
An irregular, meandering grass path cuts through the garden, forming a contrasting foil for the living walls of cow parsnip, with a froth of creamy white flower heads.

GARDEN PROFILE

ORIGINS

LOCATION: The Midlands, England.
AREA: There are a total of 150 acres (60 hectares) of flowering hay meadows.
HISTORY: Started in the mid-1970s on the original Edwardian garden layout.

SITE CHARACTERISTICS

SOIL TYPE: Neutral clay, but some areas are limy.
CLIMATE: Temperate. Average annual rainfall is 22in (550mm). Winter temperatures can drop to 16°F (-9°C); in summer, temperatures may peak at 86°F (30°C).

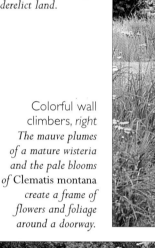

Pink corncockles (Agrostemma githago)

ORIENTATION: The garden extends to all sides of the house with a range of conditions.

SELECTED PLANT LIST

Agrostemma githago, Allium spp., Anthriscus sylvestris, Briza media, Buddleja spp., Campanula rotundifolia, Centaurea cyanus, Clematis spp., Dianthus spp., Iris spp., Laburnum spp., Lilium martagon, Linum anglicum, Lonicera spp., Narcissus spp., Ophrys apifera, Papaver spp., Philadelphus spp., Primula elatior, P. scotica, Rosa 'Etoile de Hollande', Syringa spp., Tulipa spp., Viola hirta.

A TEMPERATE DESIGN

I HAVE TAKEN the rolling, wooded landscape of the Weald of Kent in England as my starting point for this cottage garden. Here you will find fields of hops (for making beer), fruit orchards, and grazing sheep and cattle – and many of these themes are reflected in the layout. The front garden, with its traditional picket fence, contains a muddle of flowers and herbs on either side of a paved path. At the rear of the house, the path widens into a terrace, over which stands a pergola. Made from the poles that are used in the fields for the hops to climb up and over, it provides a frame for climbing plants. The fruit trees growing down one side of the house and at the rear echo the commercial crop sited on the far hillside. In spring, there are masses of daffodils in the rough grass beneath the trees.

CULTURAL INFLUENCES

The vernacular of Wealden Kent is very strong in its building structures, its agricultural field patterns, and its managed woodland and field boundaries. White painted, wooden-fronted cottages are a particular feature of the region.

Oast house for drying hops

Hay bales after the harvest

Wealden cottage with picket fence, Kent

Hops growing on wire-strung hop poles

A JOHN BROOKES PLAN

The garden plan surrounds a traditional weatherboarded cottage. Half of the garden is given over to fruit trees to extend the surrounding orchard field; the garden also includes a vegetable patch.

Shelter belt of trees

Paved path

Orchard of fruit trees

Road

Cottage

Pergola for climbing plants

Vegetable patch

Lawn

Rough grass

NATURAL INSPIRATIONS

This part of England was one of the last areas of ancient woodland to be substantially cleared, although many wooded sites still remain, breaking up the predominating pattern of cultivated fields. This is a "cozy" landscape that has been worked for generations.

Sweeping downland landscape

Sheep grazing in an orchard

A bluebell wood

MAKING A GRAVEL GARDEN

INCREASINGLY, GRAVEL is being appreciated as an ecologically sound alternative to lawn – no watering or mowing – and an intermediate texture between hard paving and soft plants.

It reduces evaporation from the soil and, being a well-drained medium for planting, it allows seeds and seedlings to overwinter without rotting off as they might in a heavier medium.

LAYING A GRAVEL AREA

When laying gravel, it is important to prepare a level and well-compacted subbase. It is vital to clear the ground of any weeds, then remove a thin, even layer of topsoil for use elsewhere in the garden. In a small area, you can gauge this by eye; in a large plot, use a level and straightedge to check that the base is level.

1 Digging out the area
Remove a 4in (10cm) layer of soil from the area. Edge the area with bricks in mortar or treated lumber, or let it merge into a flowerbed.

2 Preparing the base
Level the ground, then fill the excavated area with roughly processed gravel up to the original height. Rake it completely flat.

3 Consolidating the base
Using a heavy garden roller or motorized compactor, compress the base to remove air pockets and provide a stable base.

4 Adding the gravel
Once the base is compacted to at least ¾in (2cm) below the edge, add the gravel, starting at one side and spreading it as you go.

5 Leveling the gravel
Using a rake or stiff broom, work over the area to create an even surface that is level with the retaining edge.

6 Ready for planting
Rolling the gravel will reduce movement. The area is now ready for planting (see box, above right).

DIFFERENT TYPES OF GRAVEL

Most gravels are chips obtained from a parent rock. Naturally occurring gravel, such as pea gravel and rockfines (stone dust), has been rounded by the action of water and then dredged.

Rockfines (stone dust)
This fine, dredged gravel gives a surface that can be raked into a pattern. Pea gravel has larger stones.

Granite gravel
Black granite chips give a more formal look than dredged gravels but can be somber in large areas.

Limestone chips
These come in a range of colors depending on the original rock. Use chips made from local limestone.

Coarse-gauge stone
Larger gravel, made from local stone, can be used alone or mixed with similar finer chips.

PLANTING IN GRAVEL

Gravel provides a well-drained growing medium that is especially suitable for drought-tolerant plants. The medium allows plants to self-seed and spread themselves in natural drifts, blurring the line between paths and borders.

1 Digging the hole
First scrape the surface gravel to one side. Dig a hole slightly larger than the rootball through the base into the soil below.

2 Preparing the plant
Add potting soil to the hole. Gently tease out the plant's roots then plant it so that it is almost level with the surrounding gravel.

3 Firming in and watering
Add some of the removed soil around the rootball and firm in. Replace gravel around the crown and then water in.

SUITABLE PLANTS

Grow plants that like free-draining conditions. If you want them to spread, choose self-seeders. Herbs are excellent as they like summer heat and well-drained soil, as do many of the gray-leaved plants.

HERBS
Foeniculum vulgare
Lavandula spp. (*above*)
Rosmarinus spp.
Salvia officinalis
Thymus spp.

GRAY-LEAVED PLANTS
Dianthus spp.
Gazania spp.
Helichrysum spp.
Stachys byzantina (*above*)

SELF-SEEDERS
Alchemilla mollis
Eryngium spp.
Euphorbia spp.
Sisyrinchium spp. (*above*)
Verbascum spp.

Drifts of color, *left*
Tall mulleins (Verbascum *spp.*) *thrive in a well-drained gravel area, along with poppies* (Papaver *spp.*) *and silver-leaved* Lychnis coronaria.

TEMPERATE PLANTING

IN TEMPERATE AREAS, the natural gardener may draw inspiration from the way plants and bulbs grow in the wild – often in intermingled drifts rather than neat clumps. In the garden, you can use this idea to create naturalistic planting associations, but guide it to create a stronger effect. Below, we show a bank in my own garden, which I created using an old rubbish heap as the core. There was a natural regeneration of *Onopordum acanthium*, along with *Silybum marianum*. I drifted other semiwild plants through for a natural, yet controlled, composition.

DRIFT AND FLOW

Following nature's lead in spontaneous regeneration, you will see in the plan below how I used other material either as a contrast, as with the grasses, or in drifts to create a pleasing flow of plants. The association relies on scale, texture, and foliage color.

Bare bank (far left)
Note the frequency of plants that have naturally self-seeded.

Planting up (left)
Set out the plants in their positions before planting to check the spacing and effect.

A GRASSY BANK PLAN

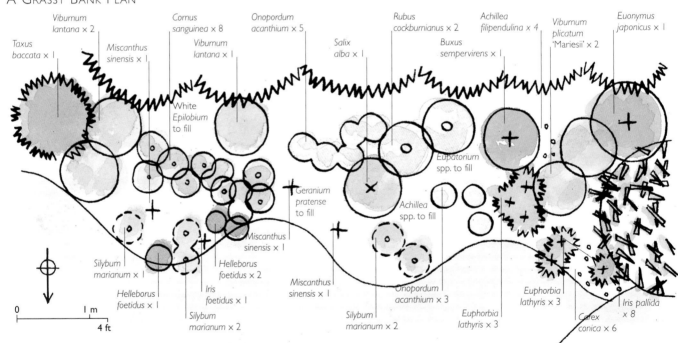

Taxus baccata × 1
Viburnum lantana × 2
Miscanthus sinensis × 1
Cornus sanguinea × 8
Viburnum lantana × 1
White Epilobium to fill
Onopordum acanthium × 5
Salix alba × 1
Rubus cockburnianus × 2
Buxus sempervirens × 1
Achillea filipendula × 4
Eupatorium spp. to fill
Viburnum plicatum 'Mariesii' × 2
Euonymus japonicus × 1
Geranium pratense to fill
Achillea spp. to fill
Silybum marianum × 1
Helleborus foetidus × 2
Iris foetidus × 1
Miscanthus sinensis × 1
Helleborus foetidus × 1
Silybum marianum × 2
Miscanthus sinensis × 1
Onopordum acanthium × 3
Silybum marianum × 2
Euphorbia lathyris × 3
Euphorbia lathyris × 3
Euphorbia lathyris × 3
Carex conica × 6
Iris pallida × 8

0   1 m
4 ft

Natural spacing
To an extent, gravel acts as a mulch, but it also allows air and space between the plant associations. The effect is much more "natural."

DRIFT AND FLOW IN GRAVEL

Here is one of my drift-and-flow plant associations in another part of the garden at Denmans (*left*). After initial planting, the subjects are allowed to self-seed or spread on their own – with an occasional edit. In this situation, plants are established in a gravel surface and are not necessarily crammed together, as in a herbaceous border, where the objective is to cover the earth with exotics before nature does it with her own materials.

PLANT EDITING

To me, plant editing is probably the most important part of gardening the natural way. It involves cutting back, thinning, or removing subjects to sustain an ongoing visual effect, while leaving enough seedheads for continuity. This form of management makes sure plants have enough space, but, most of all, it is about achieving the look I want to create. Shown below are dying circular heads of *Angelica archangelica* and the gray spikes of *Onopordum acanthium*, with masses of white-flowered *Chrysanthemum parthenium* and yellow *Tanacetum vulgare*. Poppies, *Dipsacus fullonum*, and *Oenothera biennis* will flower later in the season.

Editing for definition
Here, the editing includes cutting back the head of a viburnum among a natural planting of perennials, for better definition.

After cutting back
This semiwild border has been edited to thin out its content and let air into the grouping, with the possibility of a later show of seedlings at the front. If no plants self-seed outside the area, I plant an association to look self-seeded (inset).

NATURALIZING NARCISSUS

Tired of seeing tight little circular bunches of narcissus growing at the base of trees, I use handfuls of colorful children's building bricks to establish a naturalistic planting pattern. Narcissus will proliferate readily if they are left undisturbed.

1 Scatter colored bricks randomly
Scatter children's bricks to suggest a planting pattern.

2 Make a hole for the bulb
Make a hole 6in (15cm) deep where each brick has fallen.

3 Plant the bulb in the hole
Plant the bulb on a handful of sharp sand, then backfill and firm.

MEADOWS AND HEDGEROWS

A BROAD EXPANSE of flowering meadow with waving grasses and wildflowers is now all too rare a sight in many temperate countries. Hedgerows, too, have been another casualty of "progress" in the form of intensive, highly mechanized farming. But you can re-create these rich habitats in your own garden. It need not be a large-scale project; even the smallest garden can contain a miniature meadow. Since wildflowers generally have small leaves and flowers, the secret is to think in drifts initially – most will self-seed if you allow them to do so, and then the real excitement begins when the following year you start to get natural associations.

PLUG PLANTING A WILDFLOWER PATCH

In large or open areas, meadow plants are often sown from seed – the cheapest and most effective method for achieving a natural-looking meadow. In small or awkward patches such as on slopes, in existing turf or established planting, or between paving, it may be more practical to use small plug plants, which become established more quickly. These may be bought in trays or sown from seed in cell packs with drainage holes in the base. You may prefer to use a single species, as below, or create your own mix (see box, opposite).

1 Linking the garden with the field beyond
A tall, informal Miscanthus *grass lends importance to the gateway. It was decided to add primroses* (Primula vulgaris) *to the paved area. The best seasons for planting are autumn or spring.*

2 Making a planting hole
Using a commercial drill tool, make individual holes to take each of the plug plants.

3 Removing the plug
Water the plants well in their tray, then carefully remove each plug as needed for planting.

4 Planting the plug
Insert the plug into the prepared hole, fill around it with soil, and firm in.

5 The planted site
Plant the plugs at irregular intervals in the grass, in the gaps between paving slabs, and in the adjacent soil to create a gentle transition to the surrounding area. Water in.

SELECTED PLANTS FOR WILDFLOWER MEADOWS

Coreopsis lanceolata

Allium cernuum

MEADOW PLANTS (NORTH AMERICA)
SELECTED SPECIES FOR MEDIUM/DRY SOILS

Asclepias tuberosa (butterflyweed)
Aster laevis (smooth aster)
Baptisia australis (blue wild indigo)
Coreopsis lanceolata (lanceleaf coreopsis)
Dodecatheon meadia (shooting star)
Echinacea purpurea (purple coneflower)
Monarda fistulosa (bergamot)
Penstemon digitalis (smooth penstemon)
Petalostemum purpureum (purple prairie clover)
Rudbeckia hirta (black-eyed Susan)

SELECTED SPECIES FOR MEDIUM/MOIST SOILS

Allium cernuum (nodding pink onion)
Aster novae-angliae (New England aster)
Cassia marilandica (Maryland senna)
Heliopsis helianthoides (oxeye sunflower)
Liatris borealis (northern blazing star)

Malva moschata

Primula veris

MEADOW PLANTS (NORTHERN EUROPE)
SELECTED SPECIES FOR MEDIUM/DRY SOILS

Achillea millefolium (yarrow)
Campanula rotundifolia (harebell)
Centaurea scabiosa (greater knapweed)
Hypochaeris radicata (cat's ear)
Knautia arvensis (field scabious)
Leucanthemum vulgare (oxeye daisy)
Lotus corniculatus (bird's foot trefoil)
Malva moschata (musk mallow)
Primula vulgaris (primrose)
Prunella vulgaris (selfheal)

SELECTED SPECIES FOR MEDIUM/MOIST SOILS

Cardamine pratensis (cuckoo flower)
Filipendula ulmaria (meadowsweet)
Geranium pratense (meadow cranesbill)
Primula veris (cowslip)
Succisa pratensis (devil's bit scabious)

Established hedge
In this established laid hedge (left), the stems have been partially cut during the dormant season to stimulate the growth of new shoots. Each of the principal stems is cut up to two-thirds through (inset), at an angle to aid water runoff, then laid over to one side. Later in the season, the hedge will be a mass of green growth.

TRADITIONAL HEDGEROWS

A hedgerow provides a rich and diverse habitat for wildlife. It also filters the wind, sheltering a downwind area equivalent to 20 times its own height, so reducing soil erosion and providing protection for plants. Traditional hay meadows were usually contained by hedgerows because, after the grass was cut for hay, these fields had stock grazing on them. In the eighteenth century, fields were ditched and hedged using mainly hawthorn (*Crataegus* spp.) and/or blackthorn (*Prunus spinosa*). Over time, ways of "laying" a hedge (see above) were devised to fill out the lower areas, which tended to become bare of branches, and so escape holes were blocked.

WOODLAND GARDENS

Most of northern Europe and parts of North America were originally covered by temperate forests. These ranged from evergreen woodland, made up of firs and pines, to deciduous woods of oak, hickory, elm, beech, and ash. Much of this original forest was cleared to make way for farming, and only pockets of virgin woodland still exist; the remainder is managed. In Europe, woodland management has a long history, and includes coppiced areas (see p.99), game reserves, and other areas set aside for native plants and wildlife. Walk through your local woodland and what you see will have as much to do with human intervention as with nature. The woodland garden, too, needs management, but here the gardener seeks not to exploit but to support and nurture this special habitat.

A cool woodland glade
An open woodland garden (right) by Wolfgang Oehme and James van Sweden in Washington, DC, echoes naturally occurring glades (above).

THE SHADE GARDENER

THE DAPPLED shade of a woodland garden is its main attraction, and there are many plants that have adapted to low light levels. As well as growing shade-tolerant plants, the natural gardener can also make good use of clearings to widen the palette of species. Vegetation in wooded regions has a natural, layered order starting, in open areas, with a carpet of groundcover plants and mosses with a layer of perennials and bulbs above. Then come small trees and shrubs, and finally the tall forest standards, such as ash, oak, and beech. Dense conifers allow little growth beneath them, but in mixed or deciduous woods, spring flowers appear before the canopy is in full leaf. Man-made materials look out of place in the woodland garden; bark, wood, and stone are more sympathetic choices for any structural forms.

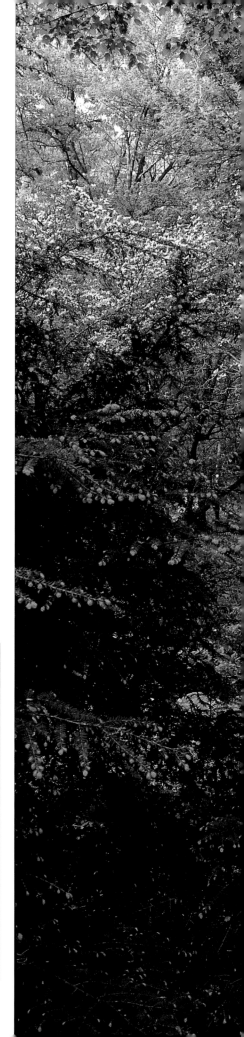

Woodland setting, *left*
The garden of landscape designer Gilles Clément embraces the natural rolling woodland of the Creuse region of central France.

Gradual transition, *below*
The ecological theme of Gilles Clément's garden gradually becomes more cultivated as one approaches the granite house.

A fallen oak provides a natural feature

CLIMATE

SEASONS: The general climatic conditions of a region are tempered in woodland. Trees modify temperature extremes, as transpiration from the leaves cools the air temperature in summer, and the shelter provides insulation in winter.

WIND: Trees provide screening from damaging winds and their drying effects.

RAINFALL: The canopy forms a filter, reducing the impact of heavy rain and snowfalls and allowing moisture to drip through to the ground below more gently.

SOIL

The pH varies, often tending to be acid because of leaf litter. Soil is usually rich in organic matter, moisture-retentive and open rather than compacted.

TERRAIN

Woodlands can be on flat terrain, slopes, valleys, or uneven ground. The landscape may include streams or pools and, in some sites, large stones or boulders.

Deciduous woodland, *above*
Shrubs grow by a stream in a natural woodland, taking advantage of the higher light levels in this natural break in the canopy.

Layered planting, *left*
In this Boston garden, dogwoods (Cornus florida) grow in dappled sun beneath the trees, underplanted with blue Phlox divaricata.

A WOODLAND SETTING

IN THE SOUTHWEST of England, sheltered valleys of native sessile oak woodland dip between high, windblown hills. At Docton Mill, where the garden includes the river, with its weir and mill race, inspired landscaping echoes the surrounding hills and valleys and has created "rooms within rooms." The effect is of a garden at peace with its woodland setting. The current gardener (not the owner), Sarah Macdiarmid, says patience is vital for the natural gardener, and advises waiting to see what grows naturally in the garden – otherwise you may never discover the treasures that are there. She also advises gardeners to take it easy on tidiness. "The urge to tidy up, deadhead, mow closely, and weed can wipe out the most interesting plants in a single season."

A wooded hollow, right
In spring, bluebells (Hyacinthoides non-scripta) and red campion (Silene dioica) appear among native ferns. Sensitive gardening has produced a successful interplay of the wild and the cultivated.

Secret steps, above
Bright yellow azaleas frame a half-hidden flight of woodland steps, overlooked by a flowering cherry tree.

A quiet corner, *left*
A wooden summer-house offers a quiet retreat in a shady wooded area planted with ferns, grasses, and brilliant rhododendrons.

Dappled glade, *right*
A shady area, edged by a stream, is planted with azaleas, maples, and pieris, with an underplanting of wild bluebells.

Banks of native ferns
A mass of ferns, including Asplenium scolopendrium, Athyrium filix-femina, *and species of* Dryopteris, *line a stretch of the river bank.*

Seasonal color
In the spring, the steep banks are filled with naturalized daffodils, primroses (Primula vulgaris), red campion, and bluebells.

GARDEN PROFILE

ORIGINS

LOCATION: North Devon, England

AREA: Approximately 8 acres (3 hectares).

HISTORY: The current owners took the garden over in 1994; previously landscaped in 1980.

SITE CHARACTERISTICS

SOIL TYPE: Mostly loam overlying clay, with some areas of almost solid clay. The pH varies from neutral through to acid.

CLIMATE: Temperate, mild, and wet. Rainfall is about 33in (830mm) a year. The ground rarely freezes in winter.

Narcissus naturalized in grass

CONDITIONS: The garden itself is remarkably sheltered, considering its location is only about ½ mile (0.8km) from the Atlantic coast.

SELECTED PLANT LIST

TREES: *Acer pseudoplatanus, Betula pendula, Crataegus* spp., *Fraxinus excelsior, Pyrus* spp., *Quercus* spp., *Sorbus* spp.

OTHER PLANTS: *Ajuga* spp., *Digitalis purpurea, Filipendula* spp., *Galium verum, Hyacinthoides non-scripta, Iris pseudacorus, Lychnis flos-cuculi, Narcissus* spp., *Primula* spp., *Prunella vulgaris, Silene dioica, Valeriana officinalis, Viola riviniana.*

A FOREST CLEARING

THE SITE OF THIS garden in the northeastern US was originally a forest of deteriorating trees. Despite the lack of light and a hard, rocky, clay soil, Lisa Mierop has created a woodland habitat whose interest extends over several seasons. Once the center of the garden had been cleared, changes of level – small mounds and undulations – were introduced, and curving paths were laid. Trees and shrubs were then reintroduced, and perennial plantings were established in areas of modified soil. Lisa Mierop is justifiably proud of her efforts. As she comments: "What I visually imagined, a naturalistic woodland garden spilling over cottage-style with lush plantings, is exactly what has been achieved."

Front garden, *above* ①
The planting at the front of the house offers an exuberant display of cottage-garden favorites such as lilies, geraniums, and salvia.

First stage: "the moon crater", *above* ②
The Mierops cleared trees to open up the garden and to let in light. The trees on the borders of the property were left to provide a framework.

Five years on: a lush shady garden, *right* ②
Despite some early setbacks, the garden is now well and truly flourishing. The process of editing initial plantings to create larger masses and groups goes on, though with each year more tree surgery is necessary to let in extra light.

GARDEN PROFILE

ORIGINS
LOCATION: The suburb of Upper Montclair, New Jersey.
AREA: About 14,500sq ft (1,350 sq m).
HISTORY: The garden was started in 1988 on a site that was overgrown and neglected.

SITE CHARACTERISTICS
SOIL TYPE: Rocky clay; in the least shady planting area, soil has been supplemented.
CLIMATE: Temperate, with four distinct seasons. Autumn brings warm Indian summer days and vivid foliage.

Perennials fill a border close to the house.

ORIENTATION: The front gets the most sun; the main garden at the rear receives little sun.

SELECTED PLANT LIST
TREES: *Betula* spp., *Cercis canadensis, Cornus florida, C. kousa, Magnolia* × *soulangeana, Picea glauca* 'Conica', *Styrax japonicus.*
SHRUBS: Species of *Berberis, Euonymus, Hydrangea, Ilex, Philadelphus, Rhododendron* (including azaleas), *Spiraea, Syringa, Viburnum.*
PERENNIALS: *Anemone* spp., *Astilbe* 'Superba', *Brunnera macrophylla, Campanula carpatica, Euphorbia polychroma, Lysimachia punctata.*

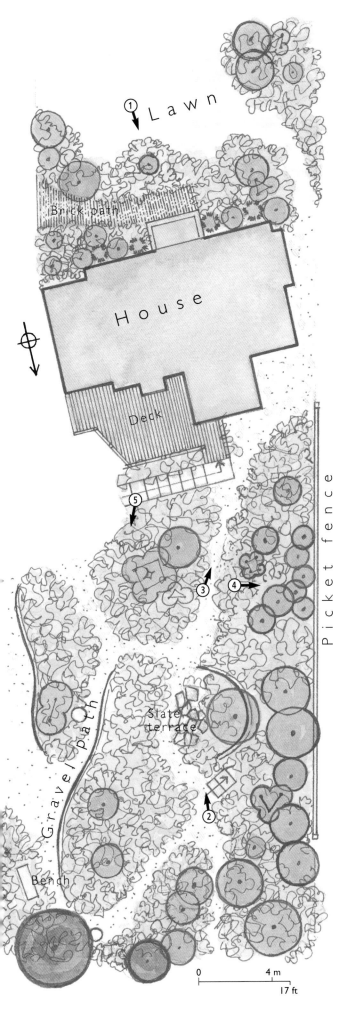

Semishady border,
above ③
*The border below the
house deck is filled
with ferns and
annuals to provide
a mixed bed.*

Cottage style, *left* ④
*White picket fencing
provides a strong
structure and a crisp
contrast to plants.*

Woodland garden
glade, *below* ⑤
*Mature oak trees and
Styrax japonicus
tower over striking
foliage plants and
groundcover, creating
a gladed effect.*

A WOODLAND DESIGN

TO DESIGN A GARDEN with a woodland backdrop seems easy, until you realize that the major shift in scale to the woodland beyond can make the garden look insubstantial and alien. This example shows you how to work with the woodland so that the feel of it sweeps into the garden, making it appear as a sunny glade. Wooden railroad ties fan out toward the house, infilled with pebbles. Beyond the planted area, the woodland floor is allowed to develop – the plants that thrive there will depend upon both the type of woodland and the density of the tree canopy in summer. The garden in spring, before the trees are in full leaf, is always a joy, with masses of woodland subjects that enjoy such a situation. Summer and autumn are more difficult, since the ground can be both dry and dark. You can improve this by adding a mulch of well-rotted leaves so that ferns can grow and, in lighter areas, introduce later interest with autumn-flowering bulbs. When the backdrop is at its greenest, the herbaceous plants, growing in full sun in the glade, will also come into their own.

CULTURAL INFLUENCES

Since earliest times, wood has been a major element in the construction of structures and buildings. In the last two centuries, industrial processes have lessened the demand, but in recent years there has been a revival of interest in and renewed appreciation of many kinds of woodcraft, from well-carved furniture to gates, stiles, wattle fences, and even woven basketwork for the garden.

Wattle fence detail

Traditional timber-built house

The author's original sketch for the garden

NATURAL INSPIRATIONS

Explore the woodland area nearest to your own location for planting ideas throughout the year. Many native plants that grow in the shade and at the peripheries will also work well in the garden.

Many ferns flourish in shade

Snowdrops emerging in late winter

Woodland in a dusting of snow

A JOHN BROOKES PLAN

A small garden in a suburban area abuts existing woodland. By going with the mood, the garden terrace seems part of a woodland clearing.

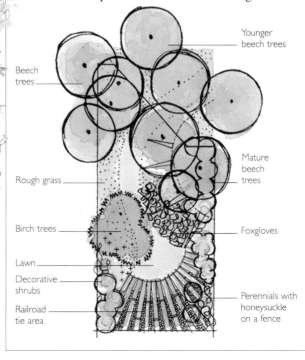

Younger
beech trees

Beech
trees

Rough grass

Birch trees

Lawn

Decorative
shrubs

Railroad
tie area

Mature
beech
trees

Foxgloves

Perennials with
honeysuckle
on a fence

MANAGING A WOODLAND GARDEN

FOR GARDENERS in temperate regions, the best examples of natural plant groupings come from the associations in clearings or at the edges of semi-natural, broad-leaved woodland. Our woodlands have been managed for generations to provide lumber and fodder, and without this intervention, they would be thick forest with nothing growing beneath the dense leaf canopy. Only with filtered light are the other layers of vegetation able to develop and create the full profile of plants from herb to tree that the gardener seeks to establish.

MAKING A NUT WALK

A nut walk is formed by planting rows of nut trees and then cutting them back to encourage them to make an arch. Hazel (*Corylus* spp.) is particularly suitable for this; seven years or so after planting, the trees are generally coppiced (see opposite) or cut back. They then quickly become multistemmed, creating a living canopy. The famous hazel Nuttery at Sissinghurst Castle in England (see right) is pruned each year to remove any unhealthy stems and excess shoots; old, well-shaped branches are left to preserve the shape.

Sketch for a nut walk
Coppiced stems and a light leaf canopy allow plants to flourish beneath. The idea is to underplant in broad drifts, perhaps with woodland bulbs and perennials for seasonal interest.

A nut walk with spring planting
At Sissinghurst Castle, the nut walk created by Vita Sackville-West is fully planted within an avenue of filberts (Corylus maxima).

COPPICING TREES

Coppicing woodland – cutting back trees almost to
ground level – stimulates regeneration and new growth.
This drastic approach to established trees is a way to
bring woodland back to the domestic scale of a garden,
while at the same time allowing in light and encouraging
new plant associations – such as spring bulbs followed by
wild flowers – to establish themselves. The word coppice
comes from the French *couper*, meaning "to cut."
Characteristic regional coppicing combinations include
hazel and ash on clay, beech and oak on sandstone, and
hazel and chestnut on well-drained land.

Cutting the tree
*This previously coppiced hazel (Corylus spp.) is being cut again. Work
around the tree in a spiral from the outside in, cutting back each stem.
Cut the stems at an angle, so that the cut slopes downward away from the
center to allow water to run off and so help prevent rot.*

2 New growth
*A hazel hedge 2–3 years after
coppicing shows vigorous new
growth. It is growing in association
with young oak trees.*

3 After five years
*The hedge is now a mass of
vertical stems. Some could be laid
laterally, interwoven with verticals,
to make a denser barrier.*

A coppiced wood in autumn, *left*
*This coppiced sweet chestnut (Castanea sativa) woodland is 14 years old.
The canopy is less dense than it would be with uncut trees, letting more
light through and allowing underlying plants and bulbs to grow.*

WOODLAND SHADE PLANTING

Many temperate woodland-floor plants have
interesting leaf shapes and coloration, the result of
their having adapted to the shady conditions, and there
is less emphasis on flower color. Beneath silver birch
(*Betula alba*) with an ivy groundcover, I put together
an association of ferns with native hellebore and
autumn-flowering cyclamen.

Positioning plants
*Before planting,
position the plants in
natural groupings.
Step back to see how
the arrangement looks
from a variety of
viewpoints, and adjust
it as necessary.*

PLANTING PLAN

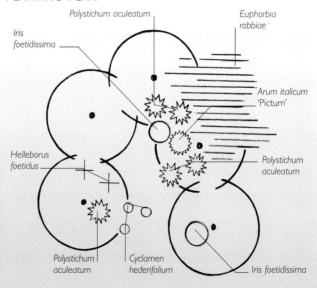

Polystichum aculeatum

*Euphorbia
robbiae*

*Iris
foetidissima*

*Arum italicum
'Pictum'*

*Helleborus
foetidus*

*Polystichum
aculeatum*

*Polystichum
aculeatum*

*Cyclamen
hederifolium*

Iris foetidissima

WORKING IN A WOODLAND GARDEN

THE CHALLENGE for the natural gardener is to create and manage the garden so that it is both practical and enjoyable, without compromising the characteristic feel of the woodland habitat. Structures such as paths and steps should be made of natural materials – especially wood – that weather well and look appropriate in a woodland setting. When choosing a tree for planting, indigenous species are in general likely to be a better choice, and to attract a greater range of wildlife, than introduced species. Native oaks are particularly good host plants; bur, red, and white oaks, for example, may support nearly 300 different insect species.

MAKING A PATH USING RAILROAD TIES

Railroad ties may be used for creating structures in the natural garden, such as for building walls and raised beds, constructing steps, or defining a pathway, as seen here. Their sizes vary, and if they have had a long and hard life, so does their condition – but all have been well treated with preservative (creosote) so that they are durable. When sawing ties, watch out for nails that may be concealed within them. If you prefer to avoid the potential health hazard of creosote in ties, you could use pressure-treated landscape timbers instead.

1 The existing site
The stepping stones through this consolidated gravel are spaced too far apart to indicate a pathway. Railroad ties will form a better link.

2 Digging the site
Scrape the surface gravel to one side and excavate the site to a depth slightly greater than that of the ties to allow for a base layer of gravel.

3 Positioning the ties
Bed the railroad ties onto the gravel in the desired pattern. Consolidate them, checking that they are level and also flush with the surrounding ground.

4 Filling in the gaps
Backfill between the ties with the excavated earth and consolidate it by firming with your heels. In dry weather, water the soil to help compact it.

5 Adding gravel
Add a layer of gravel to cover the compacted earth. Roll and consolidate it between the ties so that it is even and at the same level as the ties.

The finished path makes a distinctive yet natural-looking link between two parts of the garden.

PATHS AND STEPS

In a woodland setting, artificial materials such as brick or paving for paths and steps can look out of place. Sawn hardwood logs may be packed together vertically, retained by boards. Plants may be grown, or allowed to self-seed, in the gaps. Large cross-sections of felled trees are sometimes used as "stepping stones". Where a softer look is required, use a loose material such as bark mulch, pine needles, or woodchips.

A WOODLAND LOG PATH

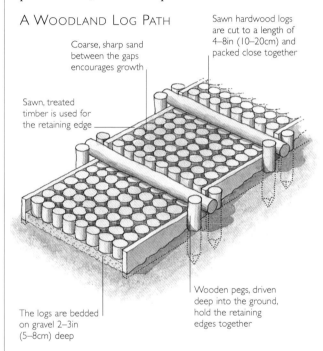

Sawn hardwood logs are cut to a length of 4–8in (10–20cm) and packed close together

Coarse, sharp sand between the gaps encourages growth

Sawn, treated timber is used for the retaining edge

Wooden pegs, driven deep into the ground, hold the retaining edges together

The logs are bedded on gravel 2–3in (5–8cm) deep

Woodland path
A path made of hardwood tree sections, sunk into the ground. These can become slippery, so use a wire brush to roughen their surface.

Forest floor
Woodchips or bark mulch are ideal for an informal path. The area can be edged with logs or allowed to run informally into the planting.

PLANTING A TREE

It is important to give a tree a good start so that it can become well established. Container-grown trees should be presoaked in their pots and the roots gently teased out before planting. When using a stake, knock it in off-center on the windward side; it should reach no more than one third of the way up the tree's stem.

1 Marking out the hole
Mark out the hole so that it is about 2-3 times the width of the rootball. Remove any turf. Dig out the hole to slightly more than the height of the rootball.

2 Scarifying the sides
In heavy soils, scarify the sides and base of the hole with a fork so that the tree's roots can spread easily. Mix the soil from the hole with well-rotted organic matter.

3 Loosening the roots
Knock in a stake, if using. Add some of the soil mixture to the hole. If you are planting a pot-bound tree, loosen the roots before positioning the tree in the hole.

4 Checking planting depth
To check that the soil is at the same level as the soil mark on the stem, lay a stake across the hole. Backfill with the soil mix, firming the soil in stages.

5 The planted tree
Water the tree well, then apply a mulch 2–2½in (5–7cm) deep around it. Secure the stake to the tree with a hose-covered wire to prevent bark damage.

WETLAND GARDENS

MORE THAN ANY other type of habitat, wetland can host an extraordinary range of plants and wildlife. For centuries, wetland areas were little valued and they were routinely drained for use as farmland or for development, being lost forever. Only now is there an increasing awareness that these are precious places that should be preserved and treasured. Any area of damp ground can be classified as wetland – marshy flats, calm pools, the damp banks of a river or stream, or a boggy area, swamp, or waterlogged ground. Distinctive characteristics depend on factors such as water depth throughout the season, speed of flow, and the type of marginal land, as well as the plants found both in the water and at its edges. If you seek to have a diversity of both flora and fauna in the garden, a water feature of some kind is vital.

Garden meets water
Located beside a saltwater inlet on Long Island (above), *this natural garden* (right) *by Wolfgang Oehme and James van Sweden fuses* Miscanthus *species grasses with native reeds at the water's edge.*

THE WATER GARDENER

THE KEY TO CREATING A natural water feature is to study examples from nature. You may wish to re-create these fairly accurately in the garden, but for maximum impact try a bolder interpretation. Large areas of water, for example, demand strong planting statements: group clumps of the same species together rather than dotting them around. Keep your planting design simple; avoid the tendency to create decorative little features with plants and stones – nature will quickly engulf them. At the same time, try to create as many different growing situations as possible by varying the soil and water depths to include a wide palette of plant material – from the handsome foliage of bog or marsh plants, to the brightly colored winter stems of wetland trees and shrubs such as willow, alder, and red-twig dogwood.

Mountain pools, *above*
Mountain streams in Colorado form a series of small pools in natural indentations in the rock, and these are quickly colonized by water-loving plants.

Garden cascade, *right*
The natural association of rock and water has been reinterpreted in this garden in Oregon to include a miniature waterfall and well-defined rocky banks.

GENERAL CONDITIONS

TYPES OF WETLAND

PONDS AND POOLS: Water is usually fairly still, allowing inclusion of floating and submerged plants as well as marginals.

RIVERS AND STREAMS: Planting depends on the current and flow. Marginals are found on damp banks.

BOGS AND WATERLOGGED GROUND: Depending on the degree of saturation, these areas may support anything from moisture-loving plants to true bog plants, which tolerate waterlogged ground.

MEADOWS AND MARSHES: Conditions vary, depending on how wet the ground is and, in meadows, whether it is wet all year round or only seasonally.

SOIL

A working definition of wetland is land where the soil is saturated for at least seven consecutive days a year and/or where the water table comes, and stays, within 12in (300mm) of the surface for seven days a year. In bogs and natural ponds, the soil is clay and typically heavy.

A naturalized Dutch water garden

Water meadow, *above*
The flat countryside of the Netherlands is punctuated by natural ponds with lush marginal plant communities.

Wetland habitat, *right*
The Dutch are pioneers in creating ecologically correct natural habitats. This lovely wetland pool is at Thijsse Park, south of Amsterdam.

A LAKESIDE VIEW

IF THE MESSAGE to the natural gardener is to "go with the flow," then this man-made lake on a Dorset estate in England is a good case in point. The idea for water came to my client one winter, when part of the surrounding grazing beyond the garden was flooded; he loved the way it provided a foreground to views of rolling farmland. Creating the lake was relatively straightforward, although after excavating the area we discovered that the water table is high at certain times of the year, and it was necessary to install a pump beneath the butyl liner to prevent it from floating. The edges of the liner were laid over a concrete rim, then backfilled with earth into the lake. This allows grass to run to the edge of the water and provides a transitional zone for marginal plants that associate with water. The many native bog plants that have since been established provide a rich habitat for wildlife.

Blending in
The house and garden now sit comfortably within their watery landscape, separated from the lake only by a low retaining wall, which was part of the original ditch (ha-ha).

DESIGN SOURCE

To work visually, the lake had to have a certain scale; too small an area of water would merely have looked like a garden pond. To demonstrate how I arrived at the swirling composition, I have laid successive traces over a photograph of the finished lake as the design progresses, taking the form of the distant landscape, its hedges and woodland, as my starting point.

1 First overlay
The line of the brow of the hill rolls into parallel lines of hedging and woodland to create a serpentine effect.

2 Second overlay
This rolling sweep is continued to provide the outline of the lake, creating bays and promontories.

3 Third overlay
The scale of the lake is established in relationship to the surrounding landscape.

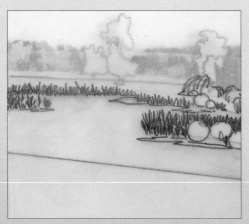

4 Finishing touches
Drifts of native plants are added to the design to create a perfect welding of new and old, with the lake merging into the existing landscape.

Natural integration, *left*
Reeds, rushes, water lilies, and
willows blend into a background
of native field vegetation.

Echoing the land, *below*
The sweep and repetition of the
landscape give way to the sinuous
outline of foreground water.

PLAN ANALYSIS

THE GARDEN AT the rear of this handsome farmhouse in England's West Country (see pp.106–107) looks out on to a formal lawn punctuated by trees, with grazing beyond for horses; from the house, the lawn and pastureland appear to run on without interruption. This visual trick is achieved by surrounding the lawn with a wide ditch, known in England as a ha-ha. This eighteenth-century device negates the need for a fence (which would impede the open outlook) to keep out livestock – the name may be a humorous reference to the fact that the ditch is invisible until, "ha-ha!", you walk right into it. The lake is sited to one side of this feature, further linking the garden with the countryside beyond.

The lake under construction ①
The cushioned butyl liner is laid over the concrete shore.

Early growth ②
Newly established marginal plants quickly soften the edges of the lake, while the mound and planting screens farm buildings adjacent to the house.

Sweeping views ③
The two cedar trees from the top lawn have subsequently been removed to open up the view of the lake from the house.

Reeds and rushes

GARDEN PROFILE

ORIGINS

LOCATION: Dorset, England

AREA: The lake is about 1 acre (0.4 hectare).

HISTORY: The garden around the house was completed in 1984–1985. The lake was constructed three years later.

SITE CHARACTERISTICS

SOIL TYPE: A thin layer of earth covered a deep vein of gravel, so deep that the local authority thought that we were digging commercially for gravel when we started excavating for the lake.

Yellow water lily (Nuphar lutea)

CLIMATE: Temperate.

ORIENTATION: The rear of the house faces southwest; the lake is situated to the west of the house.

SELECTED PLANT LIST

TREES AND SHRUBS: *Cornus alba* 'Sibirica', *C. a.* 'Spaethii', *Salix alba* 'Chermesina', *S. a.* subsp. *vitellina*, *S. caprea*, *S.* 'Chrysocoma', *S. daphnoides*.

WATER PLANTS AND MARGINALS: *Butomus umbellatus*, *Nuphar lutea*, *Typha latifolia* (cattails).

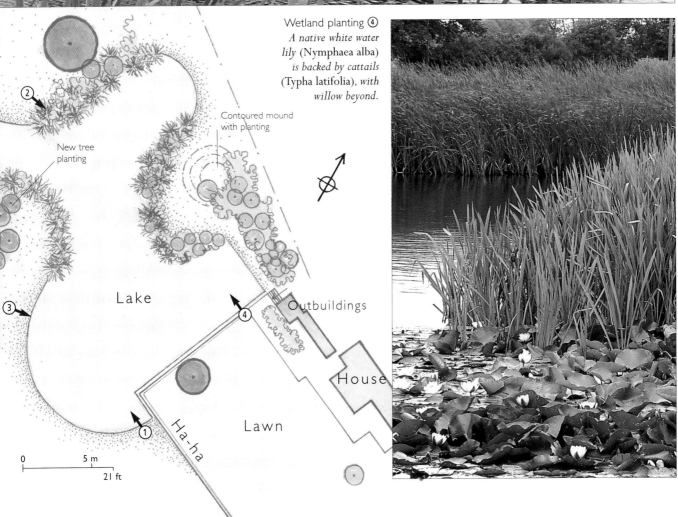

Wetland planting ④
*A native white water
lily* (Nymphaea alba)
is backed by cattails
(Typha latifolia), *with
willow beyond.*

Contoured mound
with planting

New tree
planting

Lake

Outbuildings

House

Ha-ha

Lawn

0   5 m

21 ft

A WETLAND DESIGN

I HAVE PLACED this excavated pond in a temperate wetland area that is slowly silting up and growing over. As a visual composition, a pond is usually very strong, the horizontal plane of the water contrasting with the vertical forms of the rushes and irises and perhaps the drooping outline of a weeping willow. Here, the pool gives an expanse of clear water for birds to use, as well as a habitat for damp-loving plants at the water's edge. A small island provides a haven for waterfowl where predators cannot reach them, and a decking bridge offers a good place from which to observe the wildlife. It also has the visual effect of enhancing the linear picture. Native irises and waterlilies are planted at different depths of water, and below the surface there are oxygenating plants that help keep the pool clear. At the water's edge there are plantings of *Salix* and *Cornus* species, which are coppiced each spring so that the brilliant colors of their young shoots light up the banks in winter. The effect is one of managed wildness, for a watery site in the garden always requires a certain amount of informed seasonal maintenance.

CULTURAL INFLUENCES

The "farming" of reeds and cattails and the coppicing of willow in the form of osier beds are traditional wetland practices in temperate regions. The reeds are used for thatching and the willow for various woodcrafts, including basketwork.

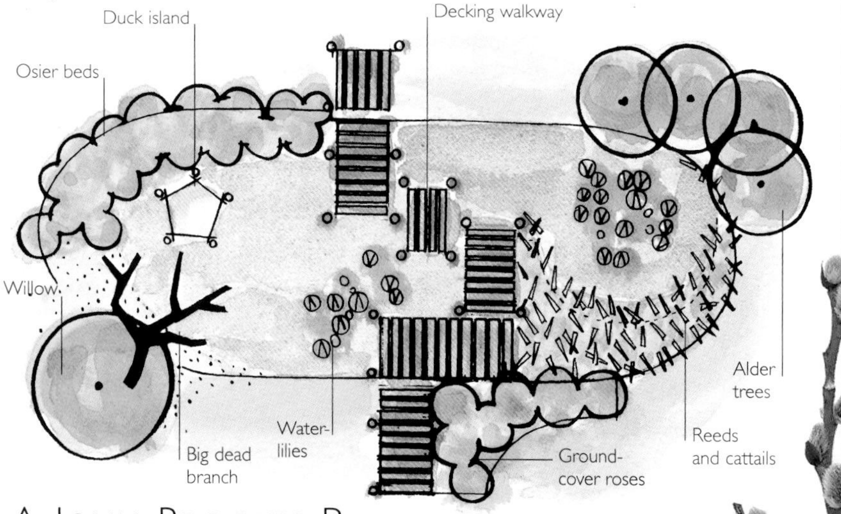

A JOHN BROOKES PLAN

Plan labels: Duck island, Decking walkway, Osier beds, Willow, Big dead branch, Water-lilies, Ground-cover roses, Reeds and cattails, Alder trees

This plan contrasts the Japanese-like feel of the decking bridge across the pond with the abundant vegetation of a temperate wetland habitat. This is an ambitious project and would require a certain amount of informed maintenance to sustain.

NATURAL INSPIRATIONS

I am very excited by plant shapes in temperate wetland, for they have great visual strength – the circular pads of waterlilies and the verticals of reeds and cattails, juxtaposed with the more subtle, and often more colorful, forms of marsh plants.

I like to exaggerate these associations in a garden by arranging them in large groupings, as seen here, which are nevertheless carefully integrated into the overall design.

Bunches of cut willow

Life focuses on the waterways in such a region

Harvesting reeds to use for thatching roofs

A marsh landscape

Reeds and waterlily pads

Iris sibirica *growing in shallow water*

NATURAL PONDS

TO PLAN AND DESIGN a natural-looking pool so that it will be in tune with its surroundings, use the local idiom as far as possible in terms of style and materials. An appropriate site for the pool is anywhere that the contours of the land form a hollow, preferably at the lowest point in the garden, which is where it would typically occur in nature. The shape of the pond, and the way you choose to edge it, will determine how well it fits into its setting. Consider whether you want a crisp distinction between pond and land, in which case choose paving, wood, or grass. For a softer, more natural effect, edge the pond with irregular pieces of rock, stone, or slate, lush planting, or a gently sloping pebble or gravel shore.

LARGER SCALE

If constructing a pond on a larger scale, use a mechanical digger. Here, a backhoe is excavating the hole for an open pond in a wetland setting. The aim is to fit the sheet of water into the landscape, with a depth and profile designed to encourage a range of wildlife.

EDGING FOR PONDS

Grass makes a most attractive edging, although there is a risk of erosion from heavy use and wildlife. Split logs, laid lengthwise or upright, give a rural effect. For a sturdier edging, you could use local stone; choose pieces that are roughly square, not neatly shaped. With grained stone, lay it so that the grain runs the same way in each piece.

STONE AND TURF

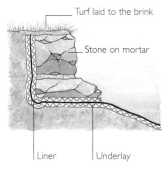

Turf laid to the brink

Stone on mortar

Liner   Underlay

A stone and turf edging, *left*
If a pond is bordered by grass, the ground must be structurally sound. To provide a stable foundation for the turf, mortar a footing of stones around the inner wall of the pond.

Grass borders
In this natural setting (below), the grass runs up to the edge of a pond. A garden pond (right) uses stone and turf to create the same effect.

First stage: excavating the site

Second stage: constructing the edge

MAKING A SHALLOW POND

To create a small pond, use a flexible membrane liner, which can be cut to size; butyl, for example, is both strong and flexible. This is best laid over cushion underlay or sand to protect the liner from sharp stones. Another layer of cushion underlay on top of the liner is advisable if you are lining the pool with stones. Hide the edges of the liner, which should be secured under a surrounding medium.

A PEBBLE BEACH EDGING

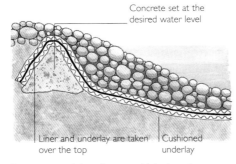

Concrete set at the desired water level

Liner and underlay are taken over the top | Cushioned underlay

Concrete edging for a pebble beach
For a strong edge, form a concrete wedge just above the water line. Lay the liner over that and then conceal it, perhaps with pebbles or cobblestones.

Digging out the shape
Dig the hole to the desired shape and depth, with shallow sloping sides. Remove sharp stones. Form a hard rim of soil at the edge to stabilize the liner.

2 Positioning the underlay and liner
First lay a cushion underlay (such as a nonwoven geotextile) to protect the pond liner, and then the liner itself. Lay pebbles around the rim, either loose or mortared in place for more stability.

3 Planting the edges
Position plants at the correct depth in concealed containers or outside the liner.

4 The finished pond
If the pond is very shallow, you may want to cover the entire base with pebbles. Make sure the edge of the liner is concealed by stones, trimming away any excess liner if necessary. Then slowly fill the pond with water. Oxygenating plants will be necessary, then snails. Don't rush to introduce fish until a balanced habitat is established.

WATERSIDE PLANTING

ONE OF THE MOST diverse habitats is to be found at the water's edge, where a wide variety of plants can flourish. Waterside plantings are probably the cheapest and easiest to achieve, and they can also be combined with other water's edge treatments (see pp.112–113) for a range of different styles. If you study natural pondside arrangements you will see that the effect, though very varied, is never staccato; plant masses drift into one another and then subtly blend into the line of the beach.

TREES AND SHRUBS

Many temperate trees and shrubs have added winter interest in the color of their stems, especially if they are regularly coppiced. Both *Cornus* spp. and willow (*Salix* spp.) have stems that vary in color from acid green through yellow and orange to brilliant red, giving double the impact when reflected in water. Willow and alder (*Alnus* spp.) are also grown for their spring catkins and, in the case of willow, their habit; the weeping willow is the classic waterside tree.

Poolside planting
Around the outer edges of the pool, marginal plants give way to water-loving shrubs and trees.

Cornus stolonifera

Salix × sepulcralis

WETLAND PLANT LIFE

Waterside plantings fall into distinct categories according to water depths. At the edge of natural wetlands there is a transitional zone between dryland and wetland plants — a boggy zone that may also be created around a garden pool by overlapping the liner with soil. In temperate wetlands a typical plant association could start with reeds and cattails whose mat of roots will seek to colonize open water, providing a footing for trees such as willow and alder. Some wetland plants are hugely invasive, and if left undisturbed will eventually dry out the marshland by raising its level. Cutting back and thinning of wetland plant material on a regular basis is therefore essential. Maintaining a large area of wetland planting may require approaching it from the water using waders, a small boat, or by dragging the pond.

BOG PERENNIALS

These plants prefer soils in which the root crown is at, or slightly above, water level for most of the time, although the level will go up and down throughout the season. They will not tolerate being submerged for long periods of time, particularly in winter.

Primula florindae

The roots of cattails (*Typha latifolia*) build up into a mat that forms a base upon which other emergent species can grow, thereby establishing the transformation from water to land.

POND CONTOURS

In the wild, the shape of a watery area will follow the contours of the ground in bold open sweeps if the water is still; if it is flowing, its outline will be more serpentine. Where there is a current running, you will see a beach on the inner side of a curve and an abrupt edge on the outer. It is getting such detail correct from the outset that will make your pond look a natural part of the landscape. Plant in bold drifts over the contours as far as is possible to emphasize the folds of the earth.

NATURAL CONTOURS

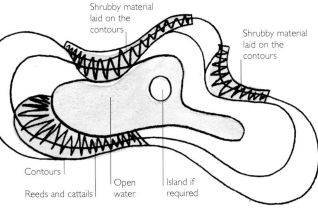

Shrubby material laid on the contours

Shrubby material laid on the contours

Contours

Reeds and cattails

Open water

Island if required

The lie of the land
A landform near water has a gentle curve to it, for in nature it is shaped by the force of the *flow if the water is a stream, or, if still, by the forces of wind and rain.*

EMERGENT AND MARGINAL PLANTS

Emergent plants are those with stems and leaves growing above the water. They are happy in a range of water depths at pool edges and in slow-running streams. In this category are marginals, which thrive with up to 12in (300mm) of water on the crown or root system. These plants, many of which are vigorous in growth, typically create the transition from land to water.

Iris pseudacorus   *Typha latifolia*

FLOATING-LEAVED PLANTS

These plants have their roots at the bottom of the pool, typically at a depth of 1–3ft (300–900mm), with their foliage floating upon the surface. In this category the best-known plants are waterlilies, which make an attractive display of leaves and flowers. The planting depth they require varies according to the species.

Nymphaea alba

SUBMERGED OXYGENATING PLANTS

These grow on the bottom of the pool and compete with algae for nutrients, keeping their growth in check. The large leaf area, which they need in order to compensate for low light levels, releases oxygen, enabling the water to support pond life. They also provide cover for fish and insects.

Ceratophyllum demersum   *Ranunculus aquatilis*

GRASSLAND GARDENS

A FAR CRY FROM the monotony of the flat, cultivated lawn, temperate grasslands are home to a great diversity of species – both grasses and native broad-leaved plants, many of which have highly colorful flowers. There are different types of grassland, including various dry prairies of the American Midwest, with undulating waves of grasses threaded through with wildflowers, the grassy plains of the South African veldt, and the flat pampas of Argentina, much of which is humid. All these regions are characterized by broad, open, rolling landscapes. True grasslands have few or no trees, so are in full sun and are often exposed to sweeping winds. Young tree seedlings find it hard to push their way through the dense grass matrix, and are further hampered by grazing, low rainfall, periodic burning, and summer drought.

Patterns of growth
*Wild pampas grass (*Cortaderia *spp.) is found in the pampas of Argentina, and also in New Zealand (above). The growth habit of this elegant plant is echoed in a grassy corner of a temperate garden (right).*

THE PRAIRIE GARDENER

Y ou can get lost in true grassland – and a feeling of wildness could be your aim when creating a garden with a prairie theme; tidiness is out of place here. The choice of plants will depend largely on the native flora and on local conditions, such as rainfall and soil type. In areas with enough rainfall, you can create a meadowlike area to border a piece of woodland (see also pp. 86–87), while in dry areas with harsher temperature extremes, a prairie garden with drought-tolerant plants would be more appropriate. Even a median strip can be seeded with a suitable mix of native grasses and wildflowers. In parts of the Midwest, a growing awareness of native habitats has even been translated into urban gardens bright with goldenrod, black-eyed Susan, and sunflowers, all at the expense of the mown lawn.

A grassy garden bank, *left*
An awkward, steep slope facing the street is transformed by an abundant prairie planting.

Flowering grassland, *above*
Bee-balm, willow-leaf sunflowers, and yellow and purple coneflowers are combined in a natural mix.

Open lands, *above*
The open, broad sweep of a rolling prairie landscape is now mostly farmland in the Midwest.

Garden context, *top*
A bold swath of Rudbeckia *species dominates this restored prairie garden in Wisconsin.*

GENERAL CONDITIONS

CLIMATE

PRAIRIE GRASSLANDS: These are found in areas with hot, dry summers and bitterly cold winters. They are unprotected by trees and are exposed to full sunlight.

PAMPAS GRASSLANDS: These have a temperate and mainly humid climate that favors the growth of pasture with tender grasses.

SOIL

QUALITY: The soil may be quite rich and well-structured, improved by the deep roots of plants and grasses, and by legumes such as clovers and vetches, which fix nitrogen in the soil.

NUTRIENTS: Beware of fertilizing the soil for new grassland, as this tends to encourage unwanted species at the expense of flowers.

Farmed prairie in Oregon

TERRAIN

OPEN LANDS: Grassland is characteristically open and in full sun. Trees and other woody plants are scarce.

SUITABLE LOCATIONS: Natural grasslands typically occur on fairly flat or broadly rolling terrain; grassy areas in gardens may also be created on banks or slopes.

ON AN OPEN PLAIN

ON A LOW KNOLL on the flat plain of the Argentine pampas stands the estate of El Choique Viejo. From the house, an expanse of mown lawn merges with the wild pampas beyond, providing an impressive panorama. In the past, I associated pampas grass with a clump on a suburban front lawn; here, seen blowing *en masse* in the wind, these flowering grasses appear as ocean waves, dotted throughout with other grasses and wildflowers. In such open spaces, wind is a constant problem, but eucalyptus – introduced by early settlers to provide shelter and to act as familiar landmarks – provides screening, punctuates the enormous plain, and the blue-gray contrasts well with flowing pampas.

A sweeping statement ②
Against the clear blue of the sky and the pool, a great drift of brilliant daylilies (Hemerocallis cultivars) provides a splash of contrasting color.

The broad horizon ①
Mown lawn, studded with acacia trees in the foreground which give shade to the house in summer, integrates the garden into the sweeping horizon beyond in spectacular fashion. The great qualities of the pampas are expressed in the negative – the absence of strident colors; the lack of sound other than the wind in the grass and sporadic birdsong; the vast, open space.

GARDEN PROFILE

ORIGINS

LOCATION: Sierra del Tandil, to the south of Buenos Aires, Argentina.

AREA: Approximately 2 acres (0.8 hectare).

HISTORY: Started on completion of the house in 1975. I first visited and made a plan in 1989, then visited again in 1994.

SITE CHARACTERISTICS

SOIL TYPE: Rich, moist, deep, slightly alkaline soil with, on this site, rocky outcrops.

CLIMATE: Continental, with temperate, wet winters and long, hot, dry summers. In the

Silvery white poplars above golden grasses

northeast of the pampas, annual rainfall is 43in (1100mm), but only 16in (400mm) in the southwest.

ORIENTATION: The property is on a slight rise, facing north (i.e. sunny).

SELECTED PLANT LIST

GRASSES: *Bromus brevis, Cortaderia selloana, Paspalum dilatatum, Spartina ciliata, Sporobolus rigens, Stenotaphrum secundatum.*

WILDFLOWERS: These appear in spring before the grasses dominate, and include species of *Oxalis* and *Oxypetalum.*

Protective trees ③

The swimming pool pavilion is sheltered by eucalyptus. Rocky outcrops contain lagunas of water.

Screening from the elements ④

Stands of white poplars have been planted close to the edge of the swimming pool to help screen it from the wind, which is a constant problem in this uninterrupted landscape.

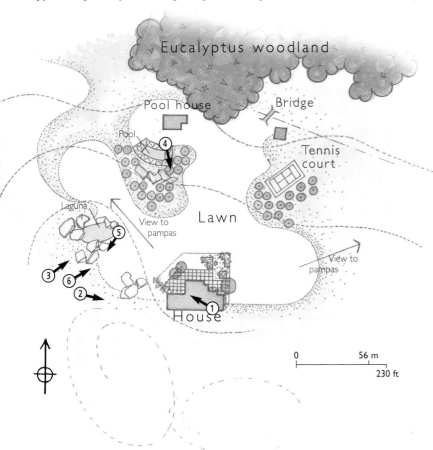

Eucalyptus woodland

Pool house

Bridge

Pool

Tennis court

④

Laguna

View to pampas

⑤

Lawn

③ ⑥ ②

View to pampas

House ①

0   56 m

230 ft

A sea of grasses ⑤

Here, the pampas has been tamed to provide an interesting garden grouping of grasses.

Rugged terrain ⑥

Outcrops of rock provide sculptural interest, while the "lagunas" (natural pools) typical of the pampas reflect the unending sky above.

PLANTING A PRAIRIE

LOOKING TODAY AT the stunning prairie garden of Neil Diboll in Wisconsin, it is hard to imagine that the site was once an untidy mass of weedy trees and shrubs. Neil, whose Prairie Plants nursery specializes in wildflowers and native grasses, spent the first two years clearing the area before seeding the prairie. He recommends sowing in the autumn to break the dormancy of many prairie seeds and thus increase germination in the spring. Five years on, his prairie garden has come into its own, and very few weeds remain. As Neil points out, the advantages of a native prairie garden, apart from its beauty, are lower maintenance, no fertilizers, very few herbicides (if any), and very low costs.

Clearing the plot, *above*
Invasive trees and shrubs were cut down, piled up, and burned.

An established prairie, *right*
Five years later, after a slow start, the prairie garden is flourishing.

Existing prairie, *above*
An original prairie remnant has been incorporated into the garden; natives include little bluestem (Schizachyrium scoparium).

Prairie and savanna, *right*
*In late summer, the garden is filled with purple coneflowers (*Echinacea purpurea)*, stiff goldenrods (*Solidago rigida)*, and rosinweeds (*Silphium integrifolium). They form a tight-knit community with prairie grasses, which effectively prevents weeds from gaining a hold. Trees associated with the Midwestern oak savanna have been allowed to stand, and these include bur oak (*Quercus macrocarpa)*, white oak (*Q. alba)*, black oak (*Q. velutina)*, and shagbark hickory (*Carya ovata).*

Autumn grasses, *above*
Big bluestem (Andropogon
gerardii) *turns red in the autumn.*

Prairie mix, *left*
Little bluestem is combined with
Bouteloua curtipendula.

GARDEN PROFILE

ORIGINS

LOCATION: South central Wisconsin.

AREA: About ½ acre (0.2 hectare).

HISTORY: The garden was designed in 1989 and sown mostly in autumn 1990.

SITE CHARACTERISTICS

SOIL TYPE: Exposed dolomite bedrock, which weathers to a thin layer of rich, dark, clay soil. Thin, sandy loam topsoil in some areas.

CLIMATE: Modified continental climate. Average annual rainfall is 30in (750mm); droughts can last for 50 days or more during

Showy goldenrod (Solidago speciosa)

the growing season. Temperatures range from as low as -40°F (-40°C) up to 115°F (46°C).

ORIENTATION: Sunny, south-facing hillside.

SELECTED PLANT LIST

FLOWERS: *Aster laevis, Baptisia leucantha, Coreopsis lanceolata, Echinacea purpurea, Eryngium yuccifolium, Lupinus perennis, Monarda fistulosa, Penstemon digitalis, Ratibida pinnata, Rudbeckia hirta, Solidago rigida.*

GRASSES: *Andropogon gerardii, Bouteloua curtipendula, Elymus canadensis, Schizachyrium scoparium, Sporobolus heterolepis.*

A GRASSLAND DESIGN

HERE I HAVE suggested a garden for a Midwestern "Prairie School of Architecture" house. The scale of the building is massive, with limestone used both in the structure of the house and its terrace walls and floor. Beneath the terrace there is a drought-tolerant fescue lawn, on either side of which are prairie plantings of wild flowers and grasses, making separate "management units." Each is mowed once in alternate years, to keep down trees and shrubs and promote the growth of the meadow plants. In a region such as this, summers can be brutally hot and dry and winters fierce and frozen. These extreme conditions have produced not only tough native plants but also strong architectural forms.

NATURAL INSPIRATIONS

It is the scale of the prairie landscape that is so amazing, with wide open spaces and an endless sky. Much of these flower-decked lands was once grazed by vast herds of bison.

Native black-eyed Susan

Native American art is often highly formalized

CULTURAL INFLUENCES

Few civilizations have identified themselves more closely with the essence of their homeland than that of the Native American people. The would-be prairie gardener can learn much from their woodcraft, their diet, and their use of medicinal plants. There has been an overlay of Western culture throughout this century, but now there is, interestingly, a return to prairie thinking.

Even farmed prairie lands are magnificent

Native American people living close to the land

A JOHN BROOKES PLAN

Plantings of prairie perennials are mixed with grasses to create a bright and loose summer effect. This contrasts strongly with the structured limestone terrace, the linear stepped walls, and the house, whose broad overhanging roof provides shade from the extreme summer glare.

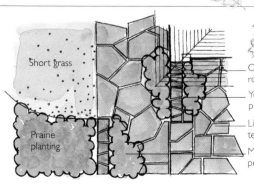

Short grass

Prairie planting

Overhanging roof

Yucca feature plant

Limestone terrace

Mixed prairie perennials

Grazing bison
on autumn
meadows

Infinite sky over
open prairie

CREATING A PRAIRIE

WHEN STARTING A PRAIRIE, the two imperatives are to make sure that the site is in full sun and to clear all unwanted vegetation, especially perennial weeds, beforehand. Include only plants that are appropriate for your soil type (you may need to have it analyzed first), and remember that, broadly speaking, the larger the plant, the more moisture it needs; dry sites will foster shorter species. Small areas can be planted with "plugs" (transplants), but this is expensive and it can be hard to achieve a really natural effect. An appropriate seed mixture includes the correct grasses as well as native wildflowers, and on any large scale this is far cheaper and the result more akin to true prairie.

TECHNIQUES AND APPROACHES

To establish a wild prairie, plantsman Neil Diboll advises scattering prairie seeds on the surface of the soil, in the autumn if possible. This encourages better germination and higher seedling survival, because germination occurs in the spring. Do not till or rake the soil, as nature will work the seeds into the soil over the winter. Neil warns against raking the soil to prepare the seedbed, since this brings up more weed seeds. Control perennial and biennial weeds that show up in the first two or three years. This is the critical period for prairie plants, so do not allow problem weeds to gain a foothold. Creating a prairie garden border is a less ambitious project, and I have devised a relatively simple plan opposite to show how this might be done. Transplants are used to combine prairie plants with garden flowers and grasses in a drift-and-flow effect (see pp.84–85) that mimics plant distribution in the wild.

ROUTINE CARE

You don't need to feed or water a wild prairie garden, but a regular patrol to remove any invasive weeds is highly advisable. Allow prairie plants to self-seed, and cut down the prairie only in late winter or early spring (this ensures vital seed food for wildlife through sparse times), then rake off the material. Although in nature the prairie might burn periodically, this can be dangerous to conduct in a domestic setting and is not recommended.

Low-maintenance garden
A wild prairie can take care of itself, but it will still need mowing once a year.

PRAIRIE PLANTING PLAN

The plan below shows the sort of planting that translates the prairie concept into domestic garden terms. It could be planted in grass or in a graveled surface. The size of each colored block approximates plant sizes in maturity. I have used both flowering perennials and grasses, all of which can be supplemented with spring bulbs. Consider using alliums, *Camassia* species, true lilies (*Lilium* species), and fritillaries.

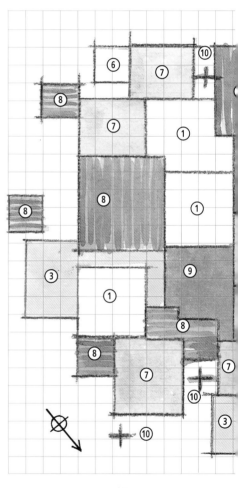

One square = 4in/10cm   ✛ = ⑩ *Allium cristophii*

Growing conditions, *above*
The ideal location for this proposed prairie-style planting is a moderately fertile, well-drained soil in full sun — perhaps a sunny bank or gentle slope. In these conditions, the plants will grow to be quite lush, and some will achieve heights of 6ft (1.8m) or more, particularly the grasses. The overall effect is intended to be reminiscent of ancient tallgrass prairie, which is now, sadly, all but extinct.

① Verbascum chaixii *f.* album
This hardy garden perennial grows to 36in (90cm).

② Eupatorium purpureum
The prairie plant Joe Pye weed can grow as high as 7ft (2m).

③ Solidago *'GoldenWings'*
Another tall prairie plant, this can reach 6ft (1.8m) high.

④ Stipa gigantea
An evergreen grass known as golden oats, it may reach 8ft (2.5m) in height.

⑤ Deschampsia cespitosa *'Goldtau'*
Tussock grass is an evergreen, with a dense, tussock-forming habit; height no more than 30in (75cm).

⑥ Koeleria cristata
A native prairie grass known as Junegrass, this perennial rarely exceeds 2ft (60cm) in height. It grows particularly well in dry, sandy soil.

⑩ Allium cristophii
This bulbous plant prefers full sun and will grow up to 12in (30cm) high.

⑨ Echinacea purpurea *'Robert Bloom'*
A garden variety of the prairie coneflower.

⑧ Miscanthus sinensis *'Silberfeder'*
Deciduous perennial grass that grows to 12ft (4m) in height.

⑦ Geranium *'Johnson's Blue'*
This herbaceous perennial will grow in most soils.

PLANTS FOR PRAIRIES

DRY, SANDY SOIL
Amorpha canescens
Asclepias tuberosa
Aster spp.
Callirhoe triangulata
Campanula rotundifolia
Coreopsis tinctoria
Echinacea pallida
Euphorbia corollata
Geum triflorum
Helianthus mollis
Liatris aspera
Lupinus perennis
Monarda fistulosa
Ranunculus rhomboideus
Rudbeckia hirta
Solidago nemoralis
Tradescantia ohiensis
Verbena stricta

GRASSES
Andropogon gerardii
Bouteloua curtipendula
Carex pensylvanica
Elymus canadensis
Koeleria cristata
Panicum virgatum

Rudbeckia hirta
Black-eyed Susan thrives on dry to medium soils.

MEDIUM SOIL
Allium cernuum
Aster spp.
Baptisia australis
Caulophyllum thalictroides
Ceanothus americanus
Desmodium canadense
Dodecatheon meadia
Echinacea spp.
Geranium maculatum
Heuchera richardsonii
Liatris aspera
Penstemon digitalis
Polemonium reptans
Ratibida pinnata
Silene regia
Silphium integrifolium
Solidago speciosa
Zizia aptera

GRASSES
Andropogon gerardii
Elymus canadensis
Sorghastrum nutans
Sporobolus heterolepis

Echinacea *spp.*
The coneflower is a prairie favorite, and will grow in a medium, well-drained soil in full sun.

MOIST SOIL
Asclepias incarnata
Aster spp.
Chelone glabra
Eupatorium maculatum
E. perfoliatum
Filipendula rubra
Gentiana andrewsii
Hypericum pyramidatum
Iris missouriensis
Liatris pycnostachya
Lilium superbum
Lobelia cardinalis
Rudbeckia laciniata
Silphium perfoliatum
Thalictrum dasycarpum
Vernonia fasciculata

GRASSES
Andropogon gerardii
Elymus canadensis
E. virginicus
Spartina pectinata

Aster cordifolius
An aster that prefers moist, fairly fertile soil in partial shade.

DRYLAND GARDENS

F ROM THE HOT deserts of the Middle East to the high, cold slopes of the Andes, about one-third of the world's land surface is one form of dryland or another. What they have in common are poor soils, low rainfall, and extremes of temperature, making cultivation difficult. A traditional domestic approach has been to try to escape the desert by making shaded courtyards or patios and filling them with alien plants that need plentiful irrigation, or even cultivating thirsty lawns. But change is afoot, particularly in the southwestern United States, where the approach is to foster a partnership with these surprisingly rich ecosystems. Here, plants such as acacias, cacti, and other succulents that have adapted to survive in such challenging conditions are used to create gardens in sympathy with their stark surroundings.

A lesson in landscaping
The magnificent landscape of the Orange River gorge, South Africa, (above) is reinterpreted in this Johannesburg garden (right) by designer Patrick Watson to provide a wild fantasy in a walled city space.

THE DESERT GARDENER

The various ecosystems found in dryland habitats are finely balanced, and it takes a certain amount of expertise to garden well in these areas. Scarcity of water is a major problem, but the gardener can improve conditions by introducing windbreaks to lessen the effects of drying winds, and mulches to reduce evaporation. In the wild, desert plants tend to be spaced out – a necessary survival tactic where the water supply is meager – and a garden design can reflect this adaption. Their distinctive textures and unusual shapes are perfectly designed to cope with life in the intense, dry heat. For example, the ribs of some euphorbias and cacti direct any available moisture to the roots, while the fleshy leaves of succulents store water for long periods. Many plants have white or silver leaf surfaces that reflect the sun.

Out in the wild west, *right*
The spectacular beauty of wild desert flowers includes Eschscholzia *species in the Santa Catalina mountains of Arizona.*

Adapted for survival, *below*
A Tucson garden brings together a range of desert plants that have evolved in different ways to cope with the dryland conditions.

Natural inspirations, *above*
Even on a small scale, a feeling of space is retained in this South African garden, with each plant self-contained. The complementary hard materials echo the textures and colors of the desert floor.

Limited resources, *right*
Because plants in desert areas must compete for what little water there is, they are often well spaced out and separate, as in this rocky plain on the African continent.

GENERAL CONDITIONS

Stark dryland beauty in West Africa

CLIMATE

RAINFALL: Drylands have less than 20in (500mm) of rain a year; true deserts less than 10in (250mm). Periods of drought may be very extensive. Some areas have periodic heavy rainstorms.

WIND: Desiccating, often sand-laden, winds increase moisture loss and soil erosion.

TEMPERATURES: These vary enormously according to site. Typically, drylands have long, hot, arid summers. In some areas, the temperature drops well below freezing at night. There may even be snow.

SOIL

Soil in dryland habitats is typically poor, low in fertility and organic matter, and very free-draining. It may have a high sand content or be very stony, and is prone to erosion.

TERRAIN

Drylands include a range of very different terrains: sandy plains, rocky plateaus, high-altitude scree, coastal deserts. They are often very open and windswept with little shelter, so most vegetation is low-growing.

| 3 |

DRYLAND GARDENS

LIFE IN THE DESERT

ONE OF THE saving graces of Tucson, Arizona, is its lack of water (very different from its neighbor, Phoenix), which means that this area has retained its desert identity. Plants that cannot survive drought and scorching summers simply perish. Here, in the Santa Catalina foothills to the north of the city, landscape architect Philip Van Wyck has created a spectacular desert garden, drawing his inspiration from a countryside dominated by palo verde trees and saguaro cacti, and cut through with natural drainage corridors, or washes. The rear garden in particular is a gallery of bold, sculptural plants: prickly pears, other cacti, and succulents such as agaves, aloes, and euphorbias. Philip's love and respect for desert plants is obvious: "Which is not to say," he points out, "that I don't use exotics or nondesert plants as well, but that is not where I start." Nevertheless, his sensitive choice of introduced species ensures that nothing looks too foreign or out of place.

Green oasis, *right*
The house seems to be part of the landscape, surrounded by shrubby foothills palo verde (Cercidium microphyllum), *desert hackberry* (Celtis pallida), *and spiny Engelman's prickly pear* (Opuntia phaeacantha).

FORM AND FUNCTION

In desert areas, where wood is scarce, the native vegetation is used for construction. The saguaro cactus (*Carnegiea gigantea*) grows slowly to 40ft (12m) or more – a striking vertical emphasis among other desert plants – and can live to be 250 years old. Early Spanish settlers used the split, dried plant as ceiling laths (now, only plants that have died naturally are used).

Saguaro cacti, the giants of the desert

Living fencing
Stems of ocotillo (Fouquieria splendens) *are cut, tied together, and stuck directly into the ground, where many take root to form a living fence. Fresh foliage appears when there is rain, and in spring bright red flowers attract hummingbirds.*

Succulents and shrubs, *left*
Catclaw acacia (Acacia greggii)
provides a backdrop for Euphorbia
and Cereus *species, and small*
clusters of golden barrel cactus
(Echinocactus grusonii).

The rear of the house, *below*
Looking along the wash, the
architectural forms of sword-leaved
agaves and fleshy cacti create an
impressive tableau of shapes.

PLAN ANALYSIS

IN THE ENTRANCE garden (see pp.132–133), much of which is a walled-in space, a natural feel has been retained by centering the design around an existing large native palo verde tree (*Cercidium microphyllum*), which also provides shade from the intense summer sun. This space is sheltered and used for evening barbecues. Arizona sandstone paving floors the area, with vernacular detailing in rough, sawn woodwork, wrought iron, and the use of stuccoed masonry. The rear garden has a more open quality, looking toward the Santa Catalina mountains, with views framed or screened by plants.

Architectural forms ①
A fleshy Opuntia ficus-indica *and ribbed* Cereus hildemannianus *form strong shapes against a wall, complemented by the sculptural barbecue area.*

Beyond the pale, *left* ②
Outside the garden, many of the same plants grow wild – palo verde, giant saguaro, and the chainfruit cholla tree.

Framed viewpoint, *above* ③
Windows in the boundary wall allow views out and provide ventilation for summer breezes.

GARDEN PROFILE

ORIGINS

LOCATION: Sonoran Desert, Arizona.

AREA: About 15,000sq ft (1,400sq m).

HISTORY: The garden was started in 1992.

SITE CHARACTERISTICS

SOIL TYPE: Fairly alkaline and low in organic matter. At the rear, the soil ranges from hardpan through clay to ledge rock and sand.

CLIMATE: Summer temperatures of 100°F (38°C) in the shade, 70°F (21°C) in winter, down to 25°F (-4°C) or less at night. Annual rainfall is approximately 12in (300mm).

Golden barrel cactus (Echinocactus grusonii)

SELECTED PLANT LIST

SHADE TREES: *Acacia smallii, Cercidium microphyllum, Prosopis alba, P. chilensis.*

SHRUBS: *Celtis pallida, Dalea frutescens, Leucophyllum frutescens, Pithecellobium flexicaule, Vauquelinia californica.*

CACTI: *Cereus* spp., *Echinocactus* spp., *Echinocereus* spp., *Ferocactus* spp., *Opuntia basilaris, O. phaeacantha, O. robusta, O. violaceae, Trichocereus* spp.

SUCCULENTS: *Agave americana, A. colorata, A. parryi, A. scabra, Aloe barbadensis, A. ferox, A. saponaria, Euphorbia* spp.

NATURAL INSPIRATIONS

I have combined palm-fringed oases with the stark beauty of cacti and succulents in this dryland garden. Water is rare in the desert, and all the more precious in the garden for that reason. Observe the many patterns in the desert.

A desert landscape in Arizona

Wind-ripple pattern in the sand

A JOHN BROOKES DESIGN

I have included shade in this desert garden, for life is often lived outside. The sound of water is introduced for coolness, with a range of colorful plants to relieve the monotony of unremitting sand and dust.

Shady palms

Grapevine *Albizia* sp.
pergola

Terra-cotta
water pitchers

Flowering
groundcover

Steps to the
rooftop

Water rill

Fountain basin

Lizard in Sonora, Mexico

MAINTAINING THE DRY GARDEN

A DEARTH OF WATER and extreme temperature shifts might seem a dull and unpromising habitat. In fact, the adaptations of plants to these extremes have produced very interesting modifications, albeit ones that are exacting in their requirements. Selecting the right plants for the right spot may take careful research. In the foothills of the Santa Catalina mountains in California, for example, the gardener may encounter a range of soils – such as hardpan, clay, ledge rock, and sand – all within a relatively small area. An extra hazard is that, compared with what lies beyond the boundary, the garden may offer a good source of vegetation to rodents, so young plants may need to be surrounded by wire mesh until they are established.

CREATING SHADE

Many plants of dryland climates require shade, and where the landscape has been stripped of its natural tree covering it is necessary to re-create the shade to regenerate the vegetation beneath. While shade can be provided by artificial structures, trees are an excellent way of giving varying degrees of shade according to their height and the density of their canopy. The scale of your site will help you decide on the size of tree or trees that you need. Remember that what grows naturally will do the job best, and never, ever, clear a site of its existing trees – they are your biggest asset.

Shady palms
Date palms in a dryland landscape create pools of filtered light, giving shade to this paved entrance forecourt.

TREES FOR PARTIAL SHADE

Jacaranda
mimosifolia
The tree can reach a maximum height of 50ft (15m).

Albizia julibrissin f. rosea
Cercidium microphyllum
Cordyline australis
Eriobotrya japonica
Eucalyptus formanii
Jacaranda mimosifolia
Ligustrum lucidum
Lysiloma microphylla
Melia azedarach
Parkinsonia aculeata
Phoenix canariensis
Pithecellobium flexicaule
Vitex agnus-castus

Cordyline
australis
This treelike palm may reach 10–33ft (3–10m).

TREES FOR DENSE SHADE

Eucalyptus
pauciflora
A dense, spreading tree growing to 70ft (20m).

Acacia spp. (many)
Albizia distachya
Casuarina spp. (various)
Cercidium floridum
Eucalyptus spp. (many)
Fraxinus uhdei
Gleditsia triacanthos
Pinus canariensis
Pinus halepensis
Populus arizonica
Prosopis chilensis
P. glandulosa
Tipuana tipu

Pinus
canariensis
This conifer may reach a towering 80ft (25m).

MINIMAL LAWN

It is understandable that people crave the cool of lush green grass when they are restricted to a desert landscape. But grass has to be regularly watered and fed to survive, and it therefore makes sense to keep the size of your green area in proportion to the amount of water available. Here I have created a small stone-edged circle of lawn, whose dimensions are directly related to the pressure of water issuing from the pop-up sprinkler at its center. The sprinkler is fed from the main water supply by an underground pipe.

SHRUB AND PERENNIAL BORDER

I have chosen evergreen, summer-flowering shrubs in white and shades of red for the border. The exception is the *Plumbago*, which brings a refreshing dash of blue. The *Nerium* is lovely, but its foliage is toxic and may irritate the skin.

Plumbago capensis

Nerium oleander

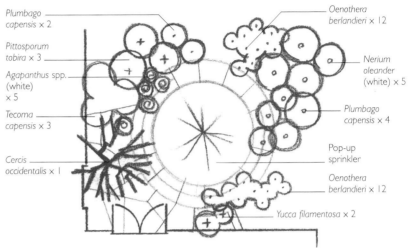

Plumbago capensis × 2

Pittosporum tobira × 3

Agapanthus spp. (white) × 5

Tecoma capensis × 3

Cercis occidentalis × 1

Oenothera berlandieri × 12

Nerium oleander (white) × 5

Plumbago capensis × 4

Pop-up sprinkler

Oenothera berlandieri × 12

Yucca filamentosa × 2

OASIS IN THE DESERT

It would be all too easy to include a vibrant blue-lined pool in a desert setting, for its harsh outline instantly adds a human dimension to this vast, uncompromising landscape. This plunge pool in the Sonoran desert, Arizona, designed by Mary-Rose Duffield, avoids such a stark contrast, and brings a feeling of the desert beyond to a garden terrace.

Terrace plunge pool
Echoing the stark landscape beyond, the pool has a strong, geometric shape and a cast concrete edging. The addition of boulders of local rock around the edge of the pool brings the beauty of the desert to a domestic setting.

CLIMBERS AND VINES FOR SHADE

An easy way to achieve shade in dryland areas is to smother an overhead structure, such as a pergola, with climbing plants. Some plants will naturally climb or cling to walls and vertical structures; others will need to be tied up frequently. Most are very rampant and will need regular pruning.

DRYLAND CLIMBING PLANTS

PLANT NAME	MATURE HEIGHT	MINIMUM TEMPERATURE
Jasminum mesnyi	10ft/3m	23°F/-5°C
Jasminum azoricum	13ft/4m	28°F/-2°C
Hoya carnosa	13ft/4m	27°F/-3°C
Plumbago capensis	13ft/4m	25°F/-4°C
Solanum jasminoides	16ft/5m	25°F/-4°C
Mandevilla suaveolens	20ft/6m	19°F/-7°C
Senecio mikanioides	20ft/6m	23°F/-5°C
Tecoma capensis	20ft/6m	17°F/-8°C
Campsis radicans	23ft/7m	17°F/-8°C
Passiflora × alatocaerulea	26ft/8m	21°F/-6°C
Thunbergia grandiflora	26ft/8m	32°F/0°C
Beaumontia grandiflora	33ft/10m	28°F/-2°C
Ficus pumila	33ft/10m	25°F/-4°C
Podranea ricasoliana	33ft/10m	25°F/-4°C
Jasminum officinale affine	33ft/10m	17°F/-8°C
Distictis buccinatoria	40ft/12m	25°F/-4°C
Macfadyena unguis-cati	40ft/12m	16°F/-9°C

MEDITERRANEAN GARDENS

THE MEDITERRANEAN REGIONS of the world are broadly distinguished by lengthy, scorching summers and long autumns with short winters and springs. The evergreen, drought-resistant plants found in these areas are ideally suited to these conditions. They tend to be shrubby, with small, textured leaves to reduce transpiration, and in the Mediterranean itself give rise to a terrain known as *macchia*, or maquis, turning to scrubland known as *garrique* where the soil is very poor. In California, this type of habitat is called chaparral, and in southern and southwest Australia it is dubbed heathland or bush. Central Chile has its *matorral*, and the Cape of South Africa its *fynbos*. Parts of New Zealand, southwest England, extreme southern Ireland, and areas of Baja California, all with highly distinctive landscapes, also enjoy a Mediterranean climate to varying degrees.

A sun-baked landscape

Olive groves stride across a hot landscape in Andalusia (above). *In this French garden* (right) *olives grow in a sea of lavender, with Spanish broom* (Spartium junceum) *behind.*

THE ARID GARDENER

If well planned, a Mediterranean garden provides year-round cover and interest. When it comes to planting in general, there's a tendency for the new gardener to the region to think no further than bougainvillea! But there is a huge range of attractive native plants to choose from that thrive in drought conditions, and these should be your first choice. However, potential problem areas – the sun, the wind, and soil erosion – must be addressed. Plants do better in semishade, so trees that filter out the sun are useful. They also help to retain moisture in the soil and prevent soil erosion. For windbreaks, rounded shrubs with small, leathery leaves, planted *en masse*, are ideal. Lawns have no place here – paved and gravel areas, echoing the natural terrain, are preferable, spot planted with ground-hugging plants for softness and color.

In the wild, *right* Olive trees are found growing wild in rocky coastal areas of the Mediterranean; groves of the cultivated trees are a common sight in many regions.

After nature, *below* Old olive trees give character to this Majorcan garden. The yellow daisy in the foreground is a form of Euryops *species with gray foliage.*

GENERAL CONDITIONS

CLIMATE

SEASONS: Hot, dry summers, long autumns, short springs and winters. Most rainfall is in the cooler part of the year. The amount of rainfall, and the severity of temperatures in summer and winter, vary depending on altitude and proximity to the sea.

WIND: Hot, dry winds off neighboring arid zones, and windburn off the sea, are a common climatic feature of these regions.

FIRE RISK: Fire is a natural hazard in these areas. However, it is also a necessary part of the ecocycle of some plants.

SOIL

Pebbly grit and rocks, with plants scattered among them, are typical. Soil erosion is a serious problem where native trees and shrubs have been uprooted and replaced by unsuitable material.

TERRAIN

Arid, sometimes mountainous, regions, generally located on the southern or western edges of major land masses.

Traditional terraced grove

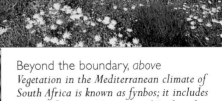

Beyond the boundary, *above*
Vegetation in the Mediterranean climate of South Africa is known as fynbos; it includes species of Protea, Ursinia, *and* Lachenalia.

Carpet of daisies, *left*
A mass of daisylike Gazania *species grow in association with several species of* Watsonia *in this natural fynbos garden in South Africa.*

HIGH UP IN THE HILLS

PERCHED HIGH in the Luberon hills of southern France is a natural garden *par excellence*, created by the late Nicole de Vésian. The key elements – clipped mounds of lavender, pencil-thin spires of cypresses, stone decorative features – take their inspiration from, and pay homage to, the surrounding landscape of rolling hills, native scrubland, and rocky terrain. The garden deliberately emphasizes the shapes and textures of this tough region, and the result is surprisingly modern while remaining true to its location. Much of what we find here is both decorative and functional. Bushy herbs such as sage, thyme, rosemary, savory, and lavender cotton are planted close together to provide a wonderful array of greens and grays; planted like this, they also conserve precious moisture. Clipping enables the gardener to explore a range of interesting shapes; but this is also Mistral country, and keeping the plants tight prevents the strong winds from tearing them apart.

A hilltop location
The garden is located on the lower terraces of a typical village in the Luberon hills of Provence. It is a very exposed site and vulnerable to rain and wind.

DESIGN INSPIRATION

One of the distinctive features of this garden is the rows of neatly clipped lavender situated on the lower terrace. Although these perfectly formed spheres may not instantly read as natural, they do in fact wonderfully echo both the worked landscapes of Provence (*left*) and the rolling hills that surround the garden on all sides. They are therefore entirely appropriate to their location.

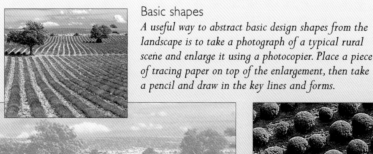

Basic shapes
A useful way to abstract basic design shapes from the landscape is to take a photograph of a typical rural scene and enlarge it using a photocopier. Place a piece of tracing paper on top of the enlargement, then take a pencil and draw in the key lines and forms.

Geometric forms
These same shapes can then be reinterpreted in the garden. Here, the decorative potential of a traditional crop of lavender is fully expressed.

Terrace garden, *left*
An old fig tree provides welcome shade from the midday sun on the top terrace.

Lavender beds, *below*
Lines of lavender play on the graphic qualities found in the commercial cultivation of the herb.

PLAN ANALYSIS

THE GARDEN CONSISTS of four terraces carved out of the rock (see pp.144–145). These are shored up by numerous dry-stone walls covered in ivy, and each level is joined by a series of steps. Areas not covered by plants are paved with flagstones or pebbles. The region offers plentiful supplies of stone, hence the strong emphasis throughout on hard features. Many of the decorative stone items, for example, have been created from discarded pieces found in nearby fields. Using mainly indigenous evergreen plants clipped into spheres, cubes, and columns, and working with a limited palette, ensures that the garden is as striking in winter as it is in summer.

Terrace garden, with seating area ①
The graphic lines and formal clipped shapes of the garden are further refined on the top terrace, linking them with the lavender beds below.

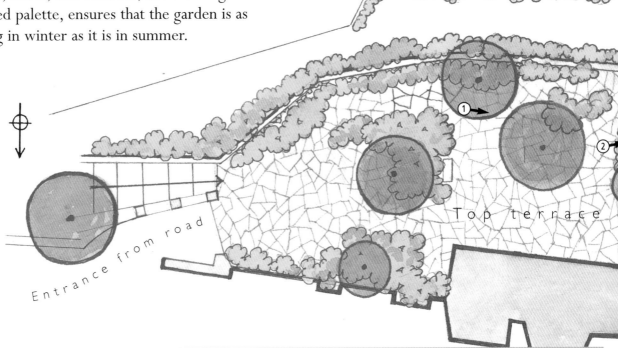

Entrance from road

Top terrace

GARDEN PROFILE

ORIGINS

LOCATION: Provence, France

AREA: Just over ½ acre (0.2 hectare)

HISTORY: When the late owner took over ten years ago, the garden had suffered from neglect and was overgrown and unkempt.

SITE CHARACTERISTICS

SOIL TYPE: Very poor, shallow soil, with solid rock often only 8in (20cm) down.

CLIMATE: Spring bright and cool, summer dry and hot, with average temperatures of 77°F (25°C). Heavy rains in late fall, followed

Beds of clipped lavender, lower terrace

by a short, cold winter; snow is usual. Prevailing winds are northeasterly.

ORIENTATION: The property sits in an exposed, windy location on a steeply sloping incline facing south-southwest.

SELECTED PLANT LIST

Ballota pseudodictamnus, Buxus spp., *Cupressus* spp., *Ficus* spp., *Genista* spp., *Lavandula* spp., *Lotus hirsutus, Rosmarinus* spp., *Salvia* spp., *Santolina chamaecyparissus, Satureja* spp., *Senecio cineraria, Teucrium fruticans, Thymus* spp., *Viburnum tinus.*

Informal herb beds, terrace garden ②
*Massed plantings of shrubby santolina and lavender carpet the upper
terrace garden, providing excellent living groundcover in lieu of a lawn.*

Scenic view from terrace garden ③
*Because of its raised position, the garden boasts many fine views of the
surrounding countryside. A small millstone sits next to yuccas in flower.*

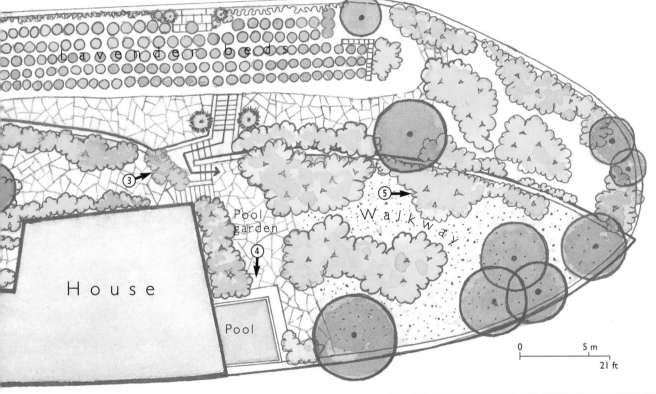

Stone pool in pool garden ④
*The south-facing wall next to the pool is home to a tender quince.
A water feature in this mainly dry landscape is particularly welcome.*

Walkway, pool garden ⑤
*Strong, sculptural shapes, including clipped shrubs, hedges, and trees,
create a boldly abstract composition in harmony with the surroundings.*

A MEDITERRANEAN DESIGN

MOST OF US have a mental image of a typical Mediterranean garden design with terra-cotta, cypress trees, and grapevines, but there are more Mediterranean regions of the world than those that border the Mediterranean Sea. This term is used to describe a type of semiarid landscape characterized by herby, small-leaved, grayish-green vegetation. For this garden, I thought that it would be interesting to relate to a similar climate – perhaps in Australia, in New South Wales, using a design inspired by the art of the Aboriginals, the First Australians. The main feature of this garden is a snake (a motif seen in many Aboriginal paintings) made of wood or concrete. The snake weaves its way through the mottled stems of established eucalyptus trees to a seating bay, with its tail finishing in a circular pool near the house. Where the foliage canopy of the eucalyptus is dense little will grow, for the ground carpet is of their shed bark, which creates a natural mulch. In lighter places, small-leaved native plants are mixed with tussock grass (*Poa habillardieri*) and morning flag (*Orthrosanthus multiflorus*).

CULTURAL INFLUENCES

Like the Native Americans, the Aboriginals lived very close to the land, and many still do. Its colors and rhythms, its fauna and flora, all form part of this culture's art, going back thousands of years. As a foreigner, outside of the country's political history, I find Aboriginal art, and modern Australian painting in general, extremely stimulating and in sharp contrast with the heritage of nineteenth-century colonialism.

Aboriginal snake painting

Vernacular tin-roofed house, New South Wales

NATURAL INFLUENCES

I think that the colors, images, and sounds of Australia are amazing – with red soils, gray plants, brilliant screaming parakeets overhead, and the strange call of the kookaburra. All of these have left me with the lasting impression of an immensely rich and varied landscape.

A koala bear

Hunter Valley vista, New South Wales

A JOHN BROOKES PLAN

My plan is of a fantasy garden, overlooked from the tin-roofed veranda. It is a gray garden, with small-leaved native shrubs and a eucalyptus canopy. A magnificent snake winds its way through the natural bark mulch and pebbly earth, and around a table.

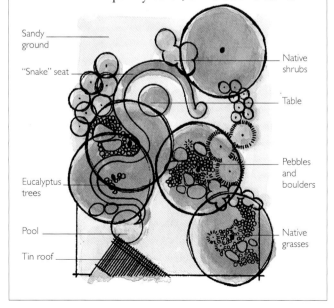

Sandy ground

"Snake" seat

Eucalyptus trees

Pool

Tin roof

Native shrubs

Table

Pebbles and boulders

Native grasses

MEDITERRANEAN GARDEN CARE

THE KEY TO creating a thriving Mediterranean garden is planning for low rainfall, soil erosion, and strong, drying winds, then selecting plants with this in mind. In these locations, many sites are not flat; learn from established regional farming techniques – such as incorporating terraces as part of the design to help reduce soil erosion. If well planned, Mediterranean-type gardens provide year-round interest, and remarkably carefree gardens result. Where the soil is poor and dry, including organic matter helps condition it and improve its water-holding capacity. Depending on where you live, creating a fire-retardant garden may also be a factor. Although bush fires in Mediterranean regions are part of the life cycle of plant regeneration, producing regular annual patterns of growth and decline, they can also destroy homes.

EFFECTIVE WATERING

Although winter rains are adequate for most Mediterranean plants, some do need extra water in summer. Try to group plants according to their needs to reduce water usage, and mulch the soil to conserve water. Grass is not a native surface cover in this climate, so consider pebbles, rocks, and paving instead of a thirsty lawn, softened by masses of ground-hugging plants and bulbs. Water in the evening so that the plants have time to absorb the water from the soil before much of it evaporates in the heat of the day.

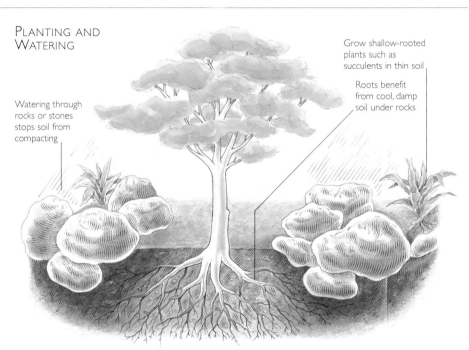

PLANTING AND WATERING

Watering through rocks or stones stops soil from compacting

Grow shallow-rooted plants such as succulents in thin soil

Roots benefit from cool, damp soil under rocks

REDUCING FIRE RISK

To prevent bush fires from destroying homes in Mediterranean areas, selected fire-retardant plant material is planted in bands to surround structures, particularly in hilly areas. Within this band (about 50ft/15m wide), medium-sized shrubs should not be used beneath trees as they tend to create a "fire-ladder." In addition, remove the lower limbs of trees, which can also act in this way. Do not plant large or flammable trees – for example cypress, eucalyptus, juniper, or pine – close to buildings in case they catch fire. Dry grass should be mown, and heavy tree litter removed from near the house and beneath shrubs.

Fire horror
Though it is a natural phenomenon, the spread of a bush fire is frightening.

FIRE-RETARDANT PLANTS

TREES AND SHRUBS
Callistemon viminalis
Ceratonia siliqua
Cistus spp.
Photina arbutifolia

CLIMBERS
Campsis radicans
Solanum jasminoides
Tecoma capensis

GROUNDCOVER
Achillea tomentosa
Gazania spp.

HILLSIDE STEPS AND TERRACES

Terracing the land into broad steps has been part of Mediterranean land management since ancient times. Depending on their location, they are planted with groves of olive, fruit, or nut trees, often against a backdrop of cypress trees, giving the region its characteristic flavor.

MULCHING PLANTS

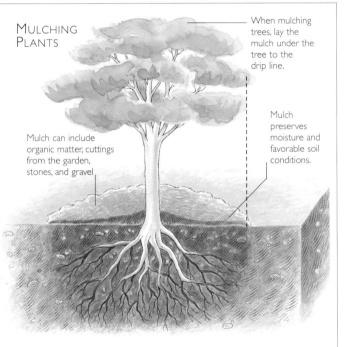

When mulching trees, lay the mulch under the tree to the drip line.

Mulch preserves moisture and favorable soil conditions.

Mulch can include organic matter, cuttings from the garden, stones, and gravel

MEDITERRANEAN STEPS

These steps, made of volcanic rock from the local region, have a simple style and grace, with built-in seating and plants fully integrated into their design. In fact, they were built by the gardener, who simply followed his feeling for the land rather than working to any particular plan.

Set in stone
The same type of rock has been used to make steps, retaining walls, and seating, creating an overall design that looks very much of its locale.

PLAN OF STEPS WITH SEATING

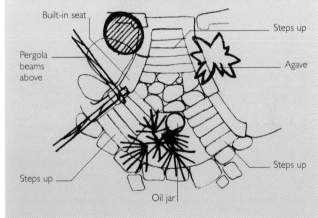

Built-in seat

Steps up

Pergola beams above

Agave

Steps up

Steps up

Oil jar

LIMITING SOIL EROSION

Along with screening the garden from wind, providing shade, and mulching heavily to reduce dehydration, stabilizing the soil is vital. On slopes, deep-rooted plants such as oleander and the carob tree (*Ceratonia siliqua*) combined with groundcovers stabilize the soil; alternatively, plant through pegged jute netting. Use local tough evergreens *en masse* for wind shelter, and native trees to cast light shade and so reduce evaporation from the soil.

STABILIZING THE SOIL

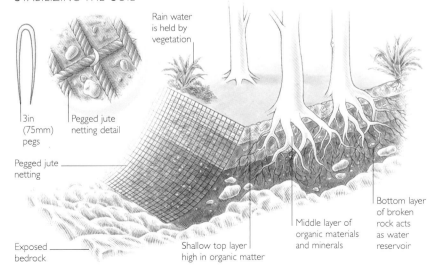

Rain water is held by vegetation

3in (75mm) pegs

Pegged jute netting detail

Pegged jute netting

Exposed bedrock

Shallow top layer high in organic matter

Middle layer of organic materials and minerals

Bottom layer of broken rock acts as water reservoir

TROPICAL GARDENS

THE WORLD'S TROPICAL regions include parts of northern and eastern Australia, southern India, Southeast Asia, southern China, Madagascar, much of the African continent, Hawaii, and from southern Mexico to Brazil. Bordering these lands are the subtropics, which encompass Florida in the United States, central South America, and parts of northern Australia. Although many of these areas have a hot and humid climate, with lush, fast-growing vegetation, this is not necessarily always the case — and rainfall and temperatures vary widely depending on altitude and terrain. Interestingly, in many hot-weather countries the idea of having a garden at all is a relatively recent European import; it is not surprising, therefore, that subtropical and tropical garden designs have tended to evolve along the traditional theme of "taming nature."

Gardens of rice
Terraced rice paddy fields (above) *are characteristic of many tropical and subtropical regions. Watercourses within a Thai garden* (right) *pick up this architectural theme. Typical steep roof lines complete the picture.*

THE EXOTIC GARDENER

In the tropics and subtropics, the indigenous plant population is typically lush. Water is plentiful in these regions, and the hot, humid climate encourages an extraordinary rate of growth. As a tropical gardener you also have the advantage of an enviable choice of plant material with which to work. This includes epiphytes such as bromeliads (members of the pineapple family), which live on other plants; rampant vines and creepers (this is the true home of bougainvillea); exotic and scented flowering shrubs, such as hibiscus and frangipani; and a vast range of flowering trees. However, the heavy rainfall can also present the gardener with a problem, quickly turning an unattended area into swampland and attracting wildlife that may not be desirable in a domestic setting, so good drainage is a priority of basic tropical garden design.

Abundant growth, *above*
Exaggerated leaf forms are a dominant feature of tropical regions; in this lushly planted Singapore garden, they have been combined to striking effect.

Tropical rainforest, *left*
The climatic conditions in the tropics and subtropics rapidly produce extremely dense growth, offering the gardener quick results.

Subtropical hammock, *above*
On areas of drier, raised land, or hammocks, evergreen hardwood trees grow with various other forms of vegetation in Florida.

Subtropical garden, *left*
Monstera deliciosa *clambers up a garden tree in Florida in its quest to reach the sunlight.*

GENERAL CONDITIONS

CLIMATE

TROPICS: Temperatures are high throughout the year, and rainfall is frequent and heavy. Plants grow at an enormous rate in this sultry climate, and their growth pattern is mostly vertical. In the rainforest, the foliage of tall trees creates a thick canopy, and many plants must climb in order to gain access to sunlight. The diversity of species in this unique environment is more varied than anywhere else on earth.

SUBTROPICS: These are the regions that border tropical areas. The climate is generally more clement, with hot, drier summers and mild, wet winters. Like tropical zones, these areas are characterized by luxuriant growth, with bright foliage and colorful flowers.

SOIL

In tropical and subtropical regions, the soil is generally thin and sandy; nutrients released into the soil are quickly taken up and stored by plants.

Gloriosa *sp. brightens a tropical border.*

PLANTING A PARADISE

IN HAWAII, A VERY unpromising site has been transformed into an exotic haven. When May Moir and her late husband inherited a featureless garden with open lawn, they decided to enclose it with walls to form a series of characterful private courts. Owing to the climate, plants grow rapidly in these islands, and rather than trying to impose restraint on natural profusion, the Moirs opted for a native style. One area (initially planted with orchids, until insects caused problems) now has bromeliads and ginger. Phalaenopsis orchids and lotus begonias fill a conservatory, and a moss garden overflows with white gardenias and ferns. The house is appropriately called "Lipolani," meaning "tropical heaven."

Front garden ②
In this area, bromeliads with striking forms and foliage in glowing colors hold sway. These have been chosen to provide a succession of bloom.

Entrance to the garden ①
Anyone entering the garden is greeted by a profusion of plants. A brilliant wave of tillandsias (Tillandsia cyanea) spills onto the entrance steps, lining the way up to the house. By the wall, a simple stone bench provides a place to relax and a viewpoint from which to enjoy the garden's beauty.

GARDEN PROFILE

ORIGINS
LOCATION: Nuuanu valley, Honolulu, Hawaii.
AREA: 14,000sq ft (1,300sq m).
HISTORY: Gradually landscaped and planted from the 1950s by May and Goodale Moir.

SITE CHARACTERISTICS
SOIL TYPE: Acid and sticky.
CLIMATE: Subtropical, with very high annual rainfall: 100–120in (2,500–3,000mm). Temperatures range from 58° to 90°F (14° to 33°C). Prevailing winds from the northeast, hurricanes southwest.

An exotic pink lotus (Nelumbo nucifera)

ORIENTATION: The side garden faces northeast into the prevailing trade winds.

SELECTED PLANT LIST
BROMELIADS: *Aechmea mulfordii, Guzmania* spp., *Tillandsia cyanea.*
ORCHIDS: *Phalaenopsis* spp., *Spathoglottis* spp.
FERNS: *Asplenium nidus. Platycerium* spp., *Polypodium* spp.
OTHER PLANTS: *Carissa grandiflora, Cordyline* spp., *Dichorisandra thyrsiflora, Gardenia fortunei, Heliconia* spp., *Medinilla magnifica, Nelumbo nucifera, Strelitzia nicolai.*

Plan labels: New driveway, Garage, Potting area, House, Front gate, Paved courtyard, Old driveway, puka-puka wall, Grassy sidewalk

Paved area ③
The paved courtyard to the rear of the house is covered with moss; the effect is that of a cool green room. There are ferns, blue ginger (Dichorisandra thyrsiflora), Spathoglottis orchids, and white gardenias (Gardenia fortunei).

0   4 m
17 ft

Borrowed landscape ④
The side garden is contained by what May calls a "puka-puka" wall (taken from the Hawaiian word for hole), which filters the trade winds but permits the air circulation that most bromeliads need. The wall is relatively low, allowing sweeping views of the Koolau mountains.

Tropical tree fern ⑤
The arching fronds of a Tasmanian tree fern are seen against the extraordinary powder-puff blooms of Calliandra haematocephala.

A TROPICAL DESIGN

HEAT AND HUMIDITY epitomize the ambience of the tropical garden, with lush, rampant growth and strong colors and forms. In many parts of the Far East, the decorative tropical garden was a concept introduced by homesick Europeans who had been transplanted to an area where a garden was merely a clearing in the jungle in which to grow essentials such as vegetables and grain. Consequently, the garden I have designed is an amalgam of Oriental styles. A central pool with an orchid island is surrounded by a paved terrace, and brightly colored Thai-style pavilions beneath swaying palm trees give shelter from tropical rain. An exotic climber softens the outlines of a Chinese moon gate, and the fence is bamboo. It is an exotic location, heavy with fragrance and overgrown vegetation and with enormous potential for development.

CULTURAL INFLUENCES

Thailand provided the focus for this fantasy garden, with bright lacquer painted structures that rival the exotic vegetation. In particular, I had in mind the temples, with their marvelous roof lines, rich gold ornamentation, and an abundance of abstract pattern.

Temple with gold decor

Colorful parasols

Floating market

Traditional Thai ornamentation

NATURAL INSPIRATIONS

The watery terraced fields for growing rice in the Far East provide an organic sculpted surface to the countryside. These shapes contrast with exotic foliage forms and a wealth of brilliantly colored flowers.

Large bamboo shoots

Terraced rice fields

Swaying coconut palms

A JOHN BROOKES PLAN

The plan has an abstract geometry to it, which is heavily overlaid with abundant growth. Jungle planting calls for strong design control, for growth is extraordinarily rapid in these regions and quickly takes over.

Hibiscus hedge

King palms

Tea houses

Paved area

Pool

King palms

Hibiscus hedge with bamboo fence behind

Orchid island

TROPICAL PLANTING

A GARDEN PLAN should take account of the rapid and luxuriant growth typical of tropical regions if the gardener is not to engage in a constant struggle to keep the vegetation under control. The clipped lawn, ubiquitous in temperate areas, does not adapt well to this climate, requiring a high level of maintenance. Native groundcover is much to be preferred in these conditions. Plants for elsewhere in the tropical or subtropical garden come in many wonderful shapes and guises, but orchids must get a special mention. In addition to their great beauty, many also have a delightful fragrance.

Subtropical grove
In subtropical and tropical areas, where soil quality is typically poor, there is a greater reliance on trees and groundcover plants for stability.

LAWN ALTERNATIVES

Although most grass substitutes can't be walked upon, they provide a comparable (or better) visual effect. In addition, using better-adapted plants is far more ecologically friendly. They need little looking after, discourage weeds, and prevent soil erosion during the frequent heavy rains. For sunny areas consider species of *Alternanthera, Lantana,* and *Rhoeo,* and for shady places species of *Zebrina, Episcia,* and *Scindapsus.*

A SANDY HABITAT

The appearance and growth habit of groundcover plants native to the tropics and subtropics will vary widely depending on where you live. Observe them in the wild, and then translate these into a garden setting. Here, various salt-tolerant coastal plants from the subtropical regions of North America are placed in a plant association that could work well in a sandy garden close to the ocean.

Zamia pumila

Uniola paniculata

Ipomoea pes-caprae

CULTIVATING ORCHIDS

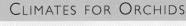

As with other plants, the original habitat of orchids provides clues to their cultivation in the garden. Account must be taken especially of temperature and humidity levels. Epiphytic orchids lodge themselves in trees, which they use for support only, gaining nutrients from organic debris at their roots – whatever is washed in by rain or dropped by birds. Those that grow in the soil are called terrestrial orchids. Most terrestrials need water throughout the year, while most epiphytes must be kept dry during part of their growth cycle. You can introduce epiphytes into the garden by attaching their roots to moss-covered bark using clear nylon thread.

Orchid and bark

CLIMATES FOR ORCHIDS

Cattleya bowringiana
This evergreen epiphytic orchid with its large, showy flowers hails from Central and South America; it is often found growing along mountain streams.

PREFERRED TEMPERATURES
COOL
50°F–70°F (10°C–21°C)
Cymbidium spp.
Odontoglossum spp.
Paphiopedilum spp. (some)

INTERMEDIATE
55°F–70°F (13°C–21°C)
Cattleya spp.
Dendrobium spp.
Oncidium spp. (some)
Paphiopedilum spp. (hybrids)

WARM
60°F–85°F (16°C–29°C)
Paphiopedilum spp. (tropical)
Phalaenopsis spp.
Vanda spp.

A DAMP HABITAT

The hot, wet conditions typical of tropical and subtropical regions mean that groundcover is quickly established in the garden, but this can be a mixed blessing, since some plants can soon get out of control and spread everywhere unless held in check. Again, observing growth habits in the wild can give you planting ideas for the garden. For example, in damp, deep wooded areas in the United States, natives such as *Mitchella repens* and *Nephrolepis exaltata* thrive in the moist, shady conditions. This association might also work well in a subtropical woodland garden.

Nephrolepis exaltata

Mitchella repens

BAMBOO BOUNDARIES

These woody-caned, perennial grasses are found in many tropical and subtropical forests and woodlands. In the garden, they are useful as hedging or as a windbreak. Choose from species of *Bambusa*, *Chimonobambusa*, and *Semiarundinaria*. Species of *Phyllostachys* make a particularly elegant screen. As the supply of bamboo is abundant, it makes a handy building material and is often used for furniture and decorative garden fencing.

Living bamboo screen

Fence constructed of fine strips of bamboo

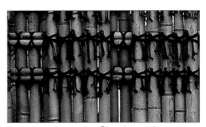

A stout screen made of bamboo poles

Bamboo poles split and tied to verticals

CITY GARDENS

THE IDEA OF natural gardening in a city might seem like a contradiction in terms. Yet towns and cities have strong regional flavors that can be reflected in gardens – it isn't hard to deduce whether you are in New York or Newcastle. Don't forget that even under paving there is soil; it may be poor, but it is there, a natural foundation beneath the artificial. Architectural clues, such as the period and style of the building, its materials, and type of paving, all mark local identity and are useful reference points for the urban gardener – brick might dominate in some areas, for example, granite or limestone in others. You may need to research your region before planning planting. In temperate areas, you don't have to re-create forest – there was also always an understory of shrubs, ferns, and grasses, which combine well with other perennials and bulbs.

Inspiration from the wild
Gravel has been substituted for lawn in a walled English garden (above), *with plants growing in a wild way through it. A London roof garden* (right) *by Dan Pearson is exuberantly planted, all in containers.*

THE URBAN GARDENER

A garden in town inevitably serves as an outside room, so consider using color on boundary walls if you have them; hues that reflect the shades of local materials, such as clay, stone, or slate, may work best, particularly if they match the house. In hot climates, adobe or terra-cotta may be used, less blinding than harsh white. Paving need not necessarily be of natural materials – concrete can look fine – but it must relate to its surroundings; soften the look with continuous planting between all the joints. The actual plant choice may vary enormously, according to region and site, but include some of the local flora. If you have a lawn, you could introduce wildflowers, even perennials, into it, or replace it with an alternative such as moss or creeping thymes. If you prefer a hard surface, add clumps of herbs for interest.

Growing natives, *left*
This Cape Town garden has native plants such as Duchesnea indica, Protea *and* Veltheimia *species.*

A blended boundary, *above*
The boundary is softened by climbers and a sumac (Rhus typhina) in an English garden.

Avant-garde solution, *above*
An architectural approach in a New Zealand garden uses cycads and a geometric lawn of thyme.

Forest planting, *top*
The planting in this subtropical garden in northern Australia echoes that of native rainforest.

GENERAL CONDITIONS

CLIMATE

TEMPERATURE: City gardens are usually warmer and more sheltered than rural areas. In many regions, gardens may be frost-free all year.
SHADE: Large, overhanging trees and adjacent buildings may cast dense shade.
WIND AND RAIN: City gardens may be sheltered from wind and also rain, due to trees and walls. Rooftop terraces are generally very exposed to all the elements.

SOIL

Soil is often poor – stony, low in fertility, and compacted – and should be improved with organic matter. The ground at the foot of a wall is often very dry, due to the effect of "rain shadow."

Exuberant colors in San Francisco

OTHER FACTORS

POLLUTION: In some areas, pollution may affect both air and soil, so choose pollution-tolerant plants.
NOISE: Traffic and street noise are often a part of urban life. Thick planting can screen out some noise and provides a psychological barrier. A fountain or water spout can add a masking distraction.

A CALM RETREAT

THE WILDER APPROACH is harder to achieve in a city garden, for the proximity of neighbors and fencing tends to impede the required effect, and the surroundings may offer little inspiration. But this wonderful garden in Washington, DC, has done it – with a controlled disarray that must surely soothe the mind far better than the mini-Versailles look so frequently found in traditional gardens. The designers, Wolfgang Oehme and James van Sweden, created a dry stream bed that gently flows through the garden, culminating in a dry "pool" at each end. In midsummer, rivulets of yellow *Coreopsis* 'Moonbeam' emphasize the sinuous form of the "stream." A millstone fountain adds sound and movement. The dry stream, the restrained use of water, and the quiet rooms inviting you to pause all contribute to an air of quiet restfulness.

Millstone fountain ①

Water from the pink granite fountain at the center of the garden bubbles up like a natural spring. To create this effect, the reservoir from which the water recirculates is hidden under a layer of stones supported by a steel grate on which the millstone fountain sits.

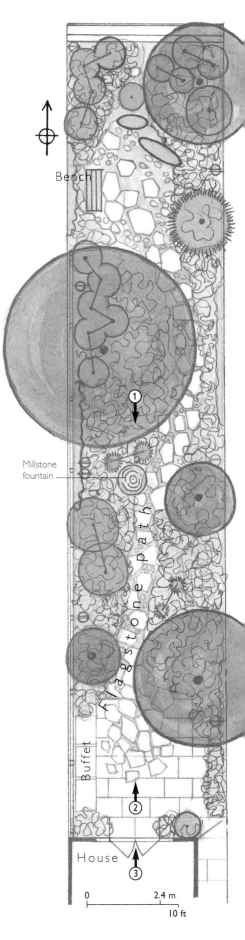

Bench

Millstone fountain

Flagstone Path

Buffet

House

0   2.4 m

10 ft

Splash of color ②
A fiery Exbury azalea, picked up by a pot-grown species of Clivia, *adds a vibrant edge to the cool green foliage. Several pots near the terrace are filled with* Lantana *species during the summer months.*

A curving pathway ③
From the garden door, a dry stream bed of flagstones set into pea gravel draws the eye to a gently sinuous line leading down the garden.

GARDEN PROFILE

ORIGINS

LOCATION: Georgetown, a section of Washington, DC.

AREA: 860sq ft (80sq m)

HISTORY: The design of the garden was started in 1991 and completed in 1992.

SITE CHARACTERISTICS

SOIL TYPE: A rich loam that typically occurs in the Georgetown area.

CLIMATE: Cold winters and hot, dry summers; this garden enjoys slightly milder conditions because of its proximity to the Potomac river.

Mazus reptans 'Albus' flows between the stones.

ORIENTATION: This north-facing garden is partially shaded but includes sunny spots.

SELECTED PLANT LIST

TREES AND SHRUBS: *Fargesia nitida, Lagerstroemia indica* 'Natchez', *Mahonia japonica* 'Bealei'.

PERENNIALS: *Acanthus hungaricus, Anemone japonica* 'Pamina', *Carex pendula, Coreopsis* 'Moonbeam', *Geranium macrorrhizum, Hosta* 'Honeybells', *Iris sibirica* 'Snowcrest', *Liriope muscari* 'Big Blue', *Mazus reptans* 'Albus', *Miscanthus floridulus, Pennisetum alopecuroides, Perovskia atriplicifolia.*

SAVANNA IN THE CITY

ONE OF THE BIGGEST objections to an urban natural garden is that it looks untidy. This was the problem that garden designer Colston "Cole" Burrell faced when he planned his ecologically sound city garden in Minneapolis. He wanted to create something that echoed the native feel of the area where woodlands, oak savannas, and prairie meet, but that was not a wild garden. Cole spent a year observing the garden first before finalizing the layout. He decided to work to a formal plan, using the shaded oak savanna grove as his main source of inspiration for the planting, and introducing lush borders reminiscent of the luxuriant growth of the prairie. The huge prairie plants, some of them 6-10ft (2-3m) tall by late summer, are not traditional, so to placate his neighbors, Cole has used grass to edge the street and front walk. "It is this conventional feature," he says, "not the exuberant array of plants, that reassures them that I am caring for the garden."

Front garden, *right*
This area gets the sun all day long, perfect for a "prairie" garden. Plants include little bluestem grass, asters, and goldenrods, with tall Joe Pye weed, Rudbeckia *'Autumn Sun', and* Silphium perfoliatum, *often known as cup plant.*

A BOG GARDEN

An artificial bog was made next to the house to receive runoff water from the roof by digging a trench 8ft x 25ft and 2ft deep (2.5m x 8m x 60cm). This was lined with strong plastic sheeting, and filled with a mix of compost and soil. It seldom needs additional water and, relying on runoff water alone, the bog can host a wide range of moisture-loving plants.

THE WATER'S ROUTE

Rainwater

A trench lined with a plastic sheet forms the bog.

Artificial bog
A number of drainage holes were made around the edge of the plastic sheeting about 12in (30cm) below the soil surface to prevent the crowns of the plants from rotting. The bog includes Astilbe *'Ostrich Plume',* Rodgersia, *yellow* Ligularia *'Zepter', and irises.*

Shaded terrace, *left*
Part of the shade garden includes meadow rue (Thalictrum spp.), *Solomon's seal* (Polygonatum hirtum), *and several types of* Geranium, *dominated by a box elder* (Acer negundo) *and* Magnolia stellata.

Container garden, *below*
The pot terrace includes wild Dicentra *species, ferns, and hostas, with agapanthus, amaryllis, ginger,* Cymbidium *orchids, and* Streptocarpus *species in pots.*

PLAN ANALYSIS

THE INTERPLAY OF the sun-filled clearing at the front of the site and the shaded "grove" formed by a multistemmed box elder at the side of the house reminded Cole of the savanna (see pp.168–169). Overlying this, the cultural inspiration for the garden grew out of Cole's image of a Midwestern farmstead – brought to mind by the courtyard area formed by the driveway in front of the garage at the center of the plot. The garden moves from open "prairie" surrounding a small lawn to a terrace bordered by a shade area and a pond feature. The rear half of the garden includes a woodland garden, a vegetable plot, and nursery beds.

Informal division ②
A Spiraea sp. hedge screens the nursery beds beyond this shady border, which includes plants such as astilbes, hostas, and epimediums.

Wide perennial borders ①
A straw path separates the nursery beds on the right, where there are hostas, epimediums, and phlox, from the tender perennial garden on the left.

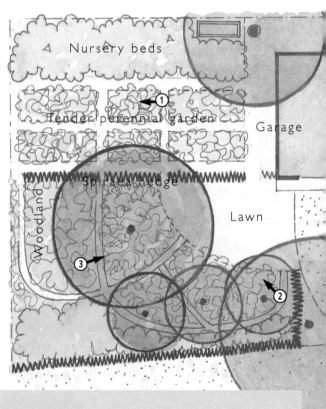

GARDEN PROFILE

ORIGINS

LOCATION: Minneapolis, Minnesota.
AREA: 9,000sq ft (860sq m).
HISTORY: The garden was started in 1991.

SITE CHARACTERISTICS

SOIL TYPE: The pH is 6.8. Silty loam to pure, fine sand in places, which dries out quickly.
CLIMATE: In winter it may drop to -34°F (-37°C) with up to five months of snow cover. Annual rainfall is 27in (680mm) but can be summer drought. Constant winds.
ORIENTATION: Mainly north-facing (i.e. shady).

The feathery goat's beard, Aruncus dioicus

SELECTED PLANT LIST

SHADE: *Actaea* spp., *Adiantum pedatum, Aralia racemosa, Asarum canadense, Cimicifuga* spp., *Claytonia virginica, Dicentra eximia, Dryopteris* spp., *Geranium maculatum, Helleborus* spp., *Iris cristata, Mertensia virginica, Polygonatum* spp., *Smilacina stellata, Viola canadensis.*

PRAIRIE: *Allium stellatum, Andropogon gerardii, Aquilegia canadensis, Aster* spp., *Coreopsis palmata, Echinacea angustifolia, Eryngium* spp., *Filipendula rubra, Geum triflorum, Heuchera richardsonii, Panicum virgatum, Penstemon gracilis, Phlox pilosa, Solidago* spp., *Verbena* spp.

Rear shade garden,
far left ③
*Ferns, irises,
pulmonarias, and
epimediums flourish
in the shade garden.*

Border, *left* ④
*The planting between
the terrace and the
driveway includes
cimicifugas, 'Purple
Cloud' meadow rue,
Lysimachia ciliata,
and Geranium
psilostemon.*

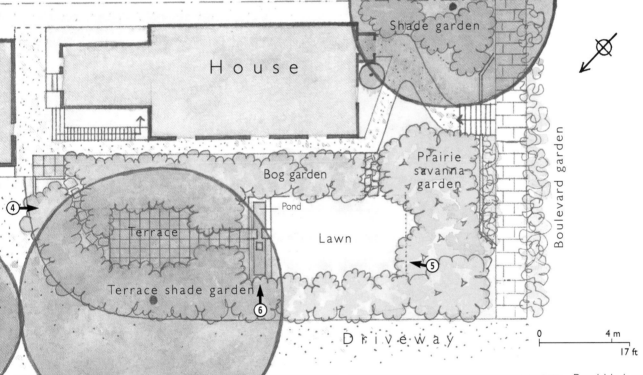

House

Shade garden

Prairie
savanna
garden

Bog garden

Pond

Terrace

Lawn

④

⑤

Terrace shade garden

⑥

Boulevard garden

Driveway

0   4 m
17 ft

Pondside border,
far left ⑤
*This includes alliums
with their seedheads
left on, hostas, blue
oat grass, baptisias,
and lambs' ears.*

Formal pond, *left* ⑥
*The structured pond
with its bridge of
paving stones provides
a strong shape to give
backbone to the
abundant planting.*

REFLECTIONS OF NATURE

I LIKE TO THINK that natural planting can overlay a Modernist design, and might expect to see this in the more progressive work on the west coast of the United States. But I was surprised to discover it in a small layout for a city garden at an English flower show – and it looks stunning. Garden designer Bonita Bulaitis has molded the space to flow between textured cast walls, opening out into a wilder space beyond, with such striking effects as a painted glass partition and a window with "rods" of water. A series of mirror-lined water channels sparkle in the sunlight; these are punctuated by intriguing circular rain pools, and the whole is softened by planting, with interweaving grasses and perennials.

Architectural plants ①
The patterns on the painted glass panels echo the forms of the sinuous grasses; these upright grasses and papyrus also help to soften the hard lines of the wall.

An outdoor room, *above* ②
Broad steps lead to a dramatically placed seating area, raised like a stage. The textured surface, a resin-bonded natural stone, offsets the mirrored pools and spilling plants.

A curtain of water, *right* ③
Water flows from a hidden tank down the outside of a series of acrylic rods, creating an unusual and fascinating water feature.

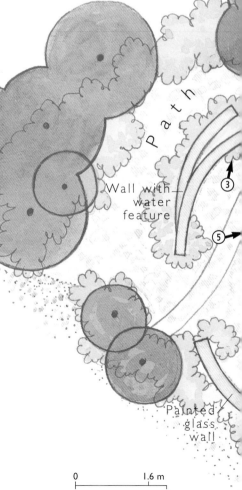

Path

Wall with water feature

③

⑤

Painted glass wall

0   1.6 m
6 ft

GARDEN PROFILE

ORIGINS

LOCATION: London, England.

AREA: 1,800sq ft (170sq m).

HISTORY: Not applicable as this is a show garden, but could be established quickly.

SITE CHARACTERISTICS

SOIL TYPE: Slightly alkaline, fairly free-draining, improved by the addition of organic matter.

CLIMATE: Temperate, in a fairly sheltered site.

ORIENTATION: An open site, largely in full sun for maximum effect from the mirrored pools and sunlight filtering through colored glass.

Painted glass partition by Susan Bulaitis

SELECTED PLANT LIST

TREES AND SHRUBS: *Acer grosseri var. hersii, Amelanchier lamarckii, Euonymus alatus, Fraxinus excelsior 'Jaspidea', Nandina domestica, Phormium tenax, Populus tremula.*

PERENNIALS: *Allium sphaerocephalon, Artemisia* spp., *Heuchera* spp., *Verbena bonariensis.*

GRASSES: *Calamagrostis acutiflora 'Karl Foerster', Carex buchananii, C. testacea, Deschampsia 'Bronze Veil', Festuca punctoria, Molinia caerulea 'Windspiel', Stipa tenuifolia.*

WATER PLANTS: *Cyperus papyrus, Equisetum hyemale, Juncus ensifolius, Scirpus cernuus.*

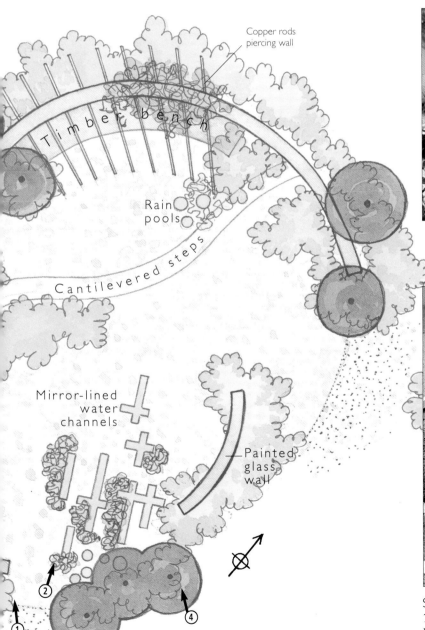

Copper rods piercing wall

Timber bench

Rain pools

Cantilevered steps

Mirror-lined water channels

Painted glass wall

Light and texture ④

Glass prisms hung in the branches of an Acer grosseri var. hersii *draw attention to its unusual bark markings.*

Serpentine lines ⑤

The sinuous curve of the resin-bonded stone steps contrasts beautifully with a clump of dark red Knautia macedonica.

A MODERNIST VIEW

ARRIVING AT THIS HOUSE cut into a Melbourne hillside was very exciting – far from being the pseudo-English garden you so often see, it was a vindication of Modernism with an overlay of natural planting. I was relieved to see that it could be done. In response to the surrounding landscape, especially the expansive views out to the Dandenong Ranges, designers Nicole Faulkner and Gregg Chapman have created a predominantly native garden under an existing canopy of eucalyptus. This is no informal "bush" garden; the sweeping stepped terraces and zigzag pool are entirely in keeping with the bold character of the house. The use of indigenous plant material is equally inspired, too. Most southeastern Australian native plants do not have showy flowers individually, but by massing species together the designers have created large drifts of interest that are in scale with the overall layout.

Entrance garden
The designers avoided taking a purist view when selecting plant material. If they could not find the right native plant in terms of size, form, texture, or color, they chose from introduced plant species.

BOLD LINES AND ARCHITECTURAL EFFECTS

The designers wanted to create a garden that would act as a setting for this striking house – which is uncompromisingly Modernist – and would look like an extension of its architecture. They used the sloping site to make a large, formal terrace and stepped levels in scale with both the house and the site. The sharp, angular lines of the house are echoed in the garden structure – in the daring zigzag shapes of the pool and paving, and in the raised beds. Large drifts of plants complement the strong lines without being overshadowed.

Main terrace, *left*
The modular look of the structure of the house is clearly visible here, and it is this dimension that has been used in the terrace design.

Terrace pool, *below*
Water was included to be cooling, as well as for visual impact. Plants such as Restio tetraphyllus *and* Brachyscome multifida *break the hard lines of the design.*

PLAN ANALYSIS

A SMALL TERRACE with a dining table forms the main entertaining space outside (see pp.174–175), which is softened by plants – a mix of species with flowers for all seasons, mostly white and pink. Existing trees provide shade and some screening from neighbors. The terrace leads down to an additional seating area, then on to a flight of stairs at right angles, edged by a hedge of *Baeckea virgata*, leading to the main terrace and lawn. One of the distinctive features of this garden is the use of scents to define different areas – the mint bushes by the front entrance are particularly fragrant after rain; on the lower lawn, the refreshing scent is of eucalyptus overhead.

Lawn

Bench

Contrast of forms ①
Muehlenbeckia complexa *is clipped to form a hedge, and provides a background to eucalyptus trunks and native wildflowers.*

Peaceful resting place ②
A quiet seating area provides the perfect spot to observe the birdlife that has returned to the garden, including bellbirds and rosellas.

Poolside planting ③
Westringia fruticosa *'Wynyabbie Gem' topiary is combined with an underplanting of cascading* Convolvulus mauritanicus.

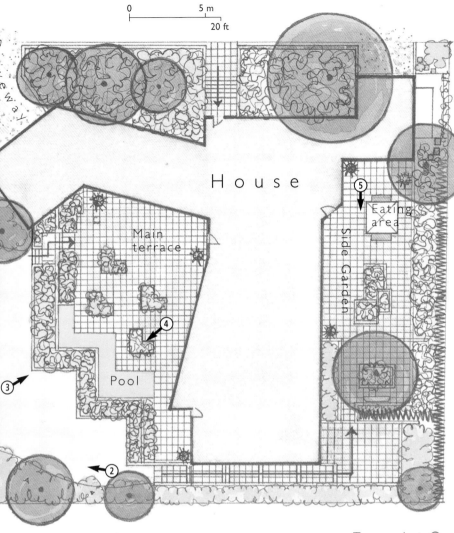

House

Main terrace

Side Garden

Eating area

Pool

⑤

④

③

②

0   5 m
    20 ft

GARDEN PROFILE

ORIGINS

LOCATION: Melbourne, Victoria, Australia.

AREA: Approximately ¾ acre (0.3 hectare).

HISTORY: Started in 1991, it took just under a year to complete.

SITE CHARACTERISTICS

SOIL TYPE: The site was mostly sticky clay with compacted builders' rubble after the house was built. Good soil was brought in for the raised beds. In other areas, such as the lawn, topsoil was incorporated. A thick, organic mulch was laid in all areas to retain moisture.

CLIMATE: Mediterranean, with hot, dry summers and cool, wet winters.

ORIENTATION: The garden faces north (i.e. sunny exposure).

Cool white Centranthus ruber *'Albus'*

SELECTED PLANT LIST

Agonis flexuosa, Baeckea virgata, Callistemon 'Reeves Pink', Choisya ternata, Cordyline australis, Eucalyptus botryoides, E. cephalocarpa, E. citriodora, E. saligna, E. scoparia, Muehlenbeckia complexa, Orthrosanthus multiflorus, Pennisetum alopecuroides, Prostanthera spp., Thryptomene saxicola, Westringia fruticosa 'Wynyabbie Gem'.

Terrace plants ④
The upright stems of blue Orthrosanthus multiflorus *soften the corners of the pool. Waterlilies also provide interest in season.*

Side garden ⑤
The west-facing outdoor eating area is flanked by masses of native and non-native plants. Doryanthes palmeri *adds height to a low bed.*

A CITY DESIGN

MY IDEA IN this imaginary garden is to bring the essence of the
Scottish countryside into town, using soft colors, sturdy plants,
and natural materials. The focal point of the simple design is a
central pool to attract birds. The gray stone of the walls reappears
here, tumbled to create a sort of scree, and around the scree is
a gravel surface of the same stone. To further enhance the wild
ambience, tufted sedges (*Carex* species) are grown in association
with heathers, and there are daisy-flowered perennials to add
interest, starting with yellow doronicum through to asters in late
summer and early autumn. Amid the brick-laid terrace, early
primroses and, later, silver thymes brighten up the surface; clematis
and honeysuckles soften the lines of the walls. The tree is a
flowering hawthorn (*Crataegus* species) to complete the rural effect.

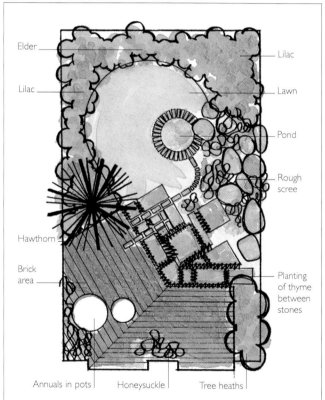

Elder —
Lilac —
Hawthorn —
Brick area —
Annuals in pots — Honeysuckle — Tree heaths —
Lilac —
Lawn —
Pond —
Rough scree —
Planting of thyme between stones —

A JOHN BROOKES PLAN

I wanted to create a focal point in this city garden
that also related to the rough scree and the
surrounding walls. My solution was to introduce
a small pond, which I then counterpoised with a
hawthorn. The wide terrace allows for an area of
outside living during the summer months.

CULTURAL INFLUENCES

In an urban location, clues to the
natural look can come from the
surrounding buildings. The use of
natural stone and the austere
architecture provide strong links
with the vigorous Scottish landscape
and the relatively harsh climate.

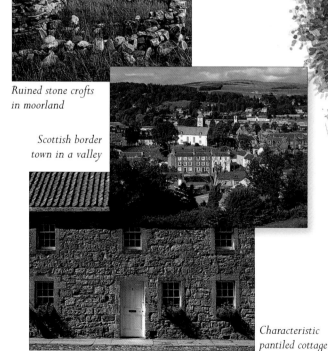

*Ruined stone crofts
in moorland*

*Scottish border
town in a valley*

*Characteristic
pantiled cottage*

NATURAL INSPIRATIONS

Moorland, wetland, sheep, and heather conjure up
Scotland in the mind's eye. These are large-scale natural
elements, the trick when creating a garden is to
transpose their essence to the domestic scale.

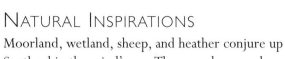

*Sweeping Scottish
moorland landscape*

*Ubiquitous purple
heather in flower*

Ever-present sheep and rain

A rugged wetland landscape

PLANTING IN POTS AND PAVING

IT IS A FALLACY that small garden spaces need small planting details – better to overscale your pots and the plants in them, and use larger trees where practical to provide a ceiling and effectively encase your outside room. Larger plots may create their own urban feel, from desert or Moorish to mysterious jungle, with a cottage-style rambling look in between. Consider also using baskets, half barrels, even pitchers as containers for your plants (but make sure that water can drain away). Think natural when selecting annuals for your tubs. Try grasses, too, and sow packets of wildflowers to mingle in with your containers.

PLANTING A WICKER BASKET

There are many handsome baskets available, and these can be used to create sympathetic containers for the natural garden. Ensure their longevity by spraying them inside and out with clear polyurethane varnish and lining them with plastic or rubber sheeting. Pierce the sheeting with holes for drainage.

1 Selecting plants
Combine plants that enjoy the same conditions. Here I have chosen a mix of fescue grasses, primroses, and dwarf narcissus for an early spring display.

2 Lining the basket
Use a sheet of black plastic to line the basket completely so that none of it will be in contact with damp soil mix, which would cause it to rot prematurely.

3 Ensuring good drainage
Make a number of holes in the liner to ensure good drainage, then add a shallow layer of coarse gravel, spread evenly out over the base.

4 Planting
Partly fill the basket with soil mix. Remove the plants from their pots and plant them, adding mix around them, so that they spill over the edges of the basket.

5 The completed basket
When the primroses are finished you can replace them with forget-me-nots (Myosotis spp.), and the narcissus with tulips.

Late summer display
For late summer interest, Coreopsis 'Moonbeam' is planted with avena grass, early single chrysanthemums, and silver thyme.

PLANTS FOR CONTAINERS

There is a huge choice of suitable plants for pots, but as they are growing in an artificial situation they will need frequent watering – some need regular feeding, too, during the growing season. Daisy-type flowers (composites) are a good choice, as they do not look too sophisticated or stiff and so fit in well with the natural look; many tolerate dry conditions and coastal sites, and will not need constant watering. In temperate areas, you can often grow Mediterranean flowers as well, but bring them under cover for winter.

A CHOICE OF DAISIES

TEMPERATE	MEDITERRANEAN
Anthemis tinctoria	Arctotis spp.
Aster spp.	Argyranthemum spp.
Chrysanthemum spp.	Brachyscome spp.
Coreopsis maritima	Dimorphotheca spp
Coreopsis tinctoria	Euryops spp.
Doronicum spp.	Eriocephalus spp.
Helenium autumnale	Erigeron spp.
Layia platyglossa	Felicia spp.
Leucanthemum maximum	Helenium spp.
Leucanthemum vulgare	Helichrysum spp.
Rudbeckia hirta	Helipterum spp.

POTS FOR PLOTS

Just as with plants, it is important to select containers that are in sympathy with their setting. As far as possible, use containers made of local, natural materials, such as wood, terra-cotta, and stone, that will complement other materials in the garden.

Rustic wooden half-barrel
This cottage-style container is filled with primroses, anemones, and spent Muscari leaves.

Traditional terra-cotta
Housed in bold terra-cotta pots, prickly pear (Opuntia species) and Cereus cactus furnish a terraced desert city garden.

PLANTING IN PAVING

In many gardens, there will be situations that require large areas of uninterrupted paving – for example, for entertaining. But too large an unrelieved expanse can look bleak in winter and be blinding in summer. Think about breaking up the surface area by introducing other hard materials to vary the texture, and further fracturing the even surface by including whatever plant material is suitable and practical for the situation.

THE RANDOM APPROACH

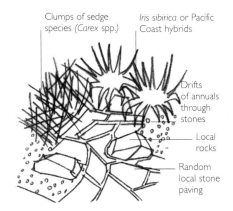

Clumps of sedge species (Carex spp.)

Iris sibirica or Pacific Coast hybrids

Drifts of annuals through stones

Local rocks

Random local stone paving

Wilder plantings look best with a random paving, possibly with rocks and drifts of self-seeded material, even between the paving joints, punctuated by irises, grasses, or sedges.

THE COTTAGE UPDATE

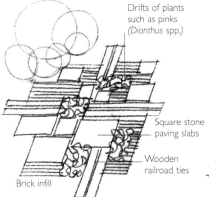

Drifts of plants such as pinks (Dianthus spp.)

Square stone paving slabs

Wooden railroad ties

Brick infill

This approach is an updated treatment of traditional cottage-garden styles and methods, using various types of hard surface with a limited, informal use of plant material.

THE SOFTER FORMAL DESIGN

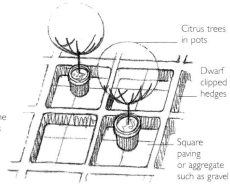

Citrus trees in pots

Dwarf clipped hedges

Square paving or aggregate such as gravel

The naturalistic, unkempt look is not suitable for an Islamic-influenced formal garden, but strips of greenery such as dwarf hedges of boxwood or lavender can relieve large-scale regularity.

ENCOURAGING WILDLIFE

WILDLIFE IN TOWN and city gardens has a fragile existence, dependent often on the goodwill of the gardener. Admittedly, in some parts of the world it is unwise to encourage wildlife into the garden. For example, in a subtropical or tropical area, shrubs and climbers that draw in birds and harmless insects may also be inviting to snakes and other undesirables, and placing such plants close to the house is to be discouraged. But temperate regions are another matter. Here, where much of the wildlife struggles to survive, any action that the natural gardener can take to provide food and shelter is welcome. Such measures tend to be reciprocal – the increased range of birds, insects, and small mammals also acts as a natural biological control, keeping down garden pests such as slugs, snails, and aphids without recourse to chemicals.

A WETLAND HABITAT

Probably the best way to encourage wildlife into your garden in temperate areas is to include a pond. It will attract a greater range of species than any other single feature. Make it as large as you can, and if possible have sloped edges or protruding rocks so that amphibians such as newts and frogs can get out easily. Flat stones at the water's edge also provide useful perching spots for birds. Lush planting by the pond's margins offers cover for small mammals and, in a large pool, waterfowl and their chicks. A wide diversity of insect life will also lure more birds into the garden. If you haven't the space for a pond, include a bird bath instead.

Trees and shrubs offer nesting sites for birds

Scented flowers attract bees, butterflies, and other nectar-feeders

Water attracts waterfowl, amphibians, dragonflies, and small insects, which in turn attract feeding bats and swallows

Foliage around edges provides shelter for chicks and small mammals

Natural garden pond, *above right*
The focus of this Dutch garden is a large, wood-edged pond generously planted both in and out of the water to provide a range of habitats.

A garden for nature, *right*
In addition to the pond, the garden offers a wide range of shrubs and trees that provide wildlife with food and shelter.

ATTRACTING INSECTS

If you want butterflies, bees, and beneficial insects that prey on pests in your garden, you need to grow flowers that are rich in nectar – often the wild species rather than the more showy cultivated plants. Try butterfly bush (*Buddleja* spp.), *Sedum spectabile*, honeysuckle (*Lonicera* spp.), herbs such as rosemary (*Rosmarinus* spp.) and lavender (*Lavandula* spp.), and many plants with daisy-like flowers (Asteraceae family) such as New England asters (*Aster novae-angliae*). Butterflies will stay in your garden if you provide sites for them to lay their eggs and food plants for caterpillars, their juvenile form – parsley (*Petroselinum* spp.) and milkweeds (*Asclepias* spp.) are particular favorites, so try to find space for them. Some insects will overwinter on herbaceous plants that have died back if they are not cut to the ground; try to save cutting back until early spring.

A magnet for insects
*Many wildflowers, including this Scots thistle (*Onopordum *sp.), are attractive to bees, butterflies and other insects. Some of these are selective feeders; for example, the Monarch butterfly (left) feeds exclusively on milkweeds (*Asclepias *spp.).*

FOODS FOR BIRDS

Trees and shrubs with berries, such as cotoneasters, mountain ashes (*Sorbus* spp.), *Euonymus* species, and hollies (*Ilex* spp.) are a valuable source of food for birds, especially in winter when food is scarce. Try not be too zealous about neatness: leave seedheads on many plants for birds to enjoy. To help them survive the winter, put out nut hangers filled with unsalted nuts or cereal flakes and provide food, including fatty foods such as bacon rind, on a bird feeder well out of reach of cats (and squirrels, if possible).

Welcome visitors
Songbirds, here an Eastern bluebird, will venture into your garden if you provide the right conditions. Try to include a range of perennials, trees, and shrubs that offer birds seeds, berries, soft fruit, or nuts, as well as shelter and protection. A water feature, however small, is another important attraction to many city birds.

NESTING SITES

Include dense or thorny shrubs and trees to provide protected nesting sites – try barberries, pyracantha, hawthorns (*Crataegus* spp.), junipers, roses, and hollies (*Ilex* spp.). A thick covering of ivy (*Hedera* spp.) on a wall or fence will also give shelter to birds, as well as small mammals and insects. Attach nesting boxes or bird houses to a tree or wall, preferably with some foliage cover around them.

Pyracantha *spp.*
These spiny evergreen shrubs bear showy autumn fruit; a favorite with many birds.

Ilex *spp.*
Many hollies bear spiny leaves; both male and female shrubs are needed to bear fruit.

Berberis *spp.*
Colorful autumn fruits are a feature of these evergreen or deciduous spiny shrubs.

INDEX

References in *italics* refer to illustrations and plans. References in **bold** include plant lists. Where the Latin and common plant names are the same, only the Latin name is used.

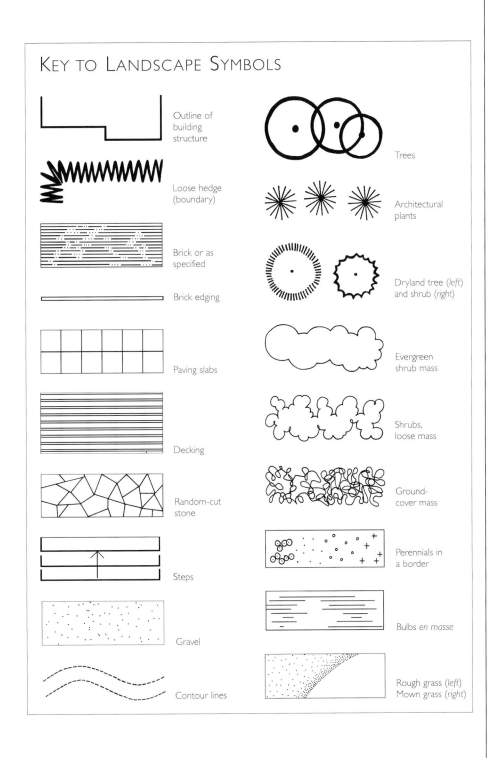

KEY TO LANDSCAPE SYMBOLS

Outline of building structure

Loose hedge (boundary)

Brick or as specified

Brick edging

Paving slabs

Decking

Random-cut stone

Steps

Gravel

Contour lines

Trees

Architectural plants

Dryland tree (*left*) and shrub (*right*)

Evergreen shrub mass

Shrubs, loose mass

Ground-cover mass

Perennials in a border

Bulbs *en masse*

Rough grass (*left*) Mown grass (*right*)

ACKNOWLEDGMENTS

AUTHOR'S ACKNOWLEDGMENTS

In putting this book together I have realized that I am only at the beginning of a journey into new gardening, which I hope many more will wish to take, each in their own individual corner of the world. I have called upon the advice and sought the help from friends along the way whom I would like to thank, in alphabetical order: Martina Barzi with Maria Josefina Casares; Sue Clifford with Angela King; Grahame Dixie; Andrew Duff and Rachel Hannibal; Heidi Gildemeister; Jim Hagstrom; Jill Hamilton; Fred and Nada Jenett; Norah Killip; Jim van Sweden; Patrick Watson; and Richard Wogisch. I would also like to thank my two colleagues at home, Michael Neve and Michael Zinn, who suffer when a book is "on the go," and my very patient secretary, Jill Robertson-Macdonald. Their help is invaluable. Additional help and long-sufferance came from my editor, Jenny Jones, who, coming from a farming background, was totally unfazed by my blending of garden with landscape. The visual aspect of the book was managed by Cath MacKenzie. I think that mix of possibility with reality was masterly. I thank both of them and their associates most warmly.

PUBLISHER'S ACKNOWLEDGMENTS

Dorling Kindersley would like to thank Claire Calman and Diana Vowles for their editorial assistance; designers Wendy Bartlet, Margherita Gianni, and Andrew Nash; Brian Craker, John Woodcock, and Chris Orr for additional illustrations; Ella Skene for the index; and models Andrew Duff, Rachel Hannibal, and Eleanor Pletts. Thanks also to Grahame Dixie of H.V. Horticulture Ltd, England, and Neil Diboll of Prairie Nursery, Wisconsin, for their invaluable advice on native plants.

We extend special thanks to Bonita Bulaitis, Mr. and Mrs. Bourcier, C. Colston Burrell, Gregg Chapman, Lionel de Rothschild, Neil Diboll, Henk Gerritsen, Janice Hall, Sarah Macdiarmid, Lisa Mierop, May Moir, Raymond Nuesch, Miriam Rothschild, Laura Stephens, Hubert de Vésian, the late Nicole de Vésian, Beryl Watson, James van Sweden, and Philip Van Wyck for supplying details of the gardens featured.

Every effort has been made to credit all the designers whose work has been featured. The Publishers would be pleased to hear from anyone who has been omitted, to whom we apologize.

FEATURED GARDENS OPEN TO THE PUBLIC

pp72–75
Priona-tuinen
Schuineslootweg 13
Schuinesloot
The Netherlands
Open to the public.

pp92–93
Docton Mill
Spekes Valley, Nr. Hartland
N. Devon EX39 6EA
England
Open to the public.

FEATURED GARDEN DESIGNERS

pp62–63
Patrick Watson Design Company
51 Muirfield Road
Greenside
Johannesburg 2193
South Africa

pp122–123
Prairie Nursery
PO Box 306
Westfield
WI 53964
US
Plants and seeds for ecological gardening, natural landscaping, and consulting services.

pp132–135
Van Wyck & Associates
627-A East Speedway Boulevard
Tucson
AZ 85705
US

pp166–167
Oehme, van Sweden & Associates, Inc.
Landscape Architects
800 G Street SE
Washington, DC, 2003
US

pp168–171
Native Landscape Design and Restoration Ltd.
407 Second Street NE
Minneapolis, MN 55413
US

pp172–173
Bonita Bulaitis, with Susan Bulaitis
Landscape and Garden Design
6 Walton Road
Ware, Herts SG12 0AA
England

pp174–177
Faulkner and Chapman Landscape Design
106 Cole Street
Brighton, Victoria, 3162
Australia

Gardens featured on pages 34–35, 76–77, 106–109 and 120–121 were designed by the author.

PHOTO CREDITS

t = top, l = left, r = right, c = centre, b = bottom, f = far, a = above, col = column

Peter Anderson: design Philip Van Wyck 25cr, 99tr, 99tc, 99ca, 99cra, 132–133a, 132–133b, 133tr, 134cl, 134cr, 134tr, 135cr, 135cb. **Arcaid**: EarlCarter/Belle /Architect A. C. Kitibutr 152–153; Mark Fiennes/Reginald Johnson 136bc; Ray Main 39br, Simon Kenny/Belle/Architect Terry Brooks 136bl. **Ardea**: J.B. & S. Bottomley: 44tr. **A-Z Botanical Collection**: 160cr. **B.C.T.V**: 67bl. **Bridgeman Art Library, London**: Corbally Stourton Contemporary Art, London: *Snake Dreaming*, 1984, Turkey Tolson Tjupurrula 148 cb. **John Brookes**: front bl, 39tr, 44bl, 61cr, 76bl, 80clb, 108cl, 108c, 113cla, 113tl, 132bc, (design Mary-Rose Duffield) 139bl, 151cra, 161br, 161crb, 161cr. **Jonathan Buckley**: design John Brookes 4fl col(iv), 5fr col(iv), 24cr, 56cl, 106c, 106cl, 106–107, 106–107c, 106bl, 106bc, 107tc, 108bc, 108–109, 109br. **Michael Busselle**: 10cb, 22–23, 28–29b, 81br, 83tr, 111bl, 140bl, 144clb, 144bl. **The J. Allan Cash Photolibrary**: 64cr, 148bl, 158cl. **Cephas Picture Library**: Mick Rock 27bl; Nick Carding 68bl. **Leigh Clapp**: (design Faulkner & Chapman) 25br, 40 /design Faulkner & Chapman 174cl, 174–175a, 174–175b, 175tc, 176, 176bl, 176br, 177bl, 177br, 177cr /design Chris Miller 60–61. **Bruce Coleman Ltd**: Alain Compost 159tc; Erwin & Peggy Bauer 149ca; Geoff Doré 65cra, 178cr; Jeff Foott productions 125tc; Jens Rydell 179cr; John Worrall 111tc; Jules Cowan 54–55. **Collections**: Michael George 71cl. **Colorific**: Peter Tenzer/Wheeler Pictures 102–103. **P. Cooper**: 49cl. **Alison Crowther**: 2–3, 47br, 48–49. **Neil Diboll**: 122br, 122cl, 122tr, 122–123, 123bc, 123cr, 123cl, 126bc; **Christine Douglas**: 4fl col(vi), 5fr col(vi), /design Philip Van Wyck 8bl, 30–31, 38–39c, 43br, 57cl /design Colston Burrell 1169tc, 170tr, 170cl, 170bc, 171tl, 171tr, 171bl, 171br. **Ken Druse**: back jacket bcl, 42bl, 90–91, 119cl. **Richard P. Felber**: design Oehme & van Sweden 102–103. **Derek Fell**: back inside flap br, 44cb, 58–59, 58bl, 160tr. **Roger Foley**: design Sheela Lampietti 96cb, /design Oehme & van Sweden, Washington 21tcr, 21tr. **F.L.P.A**: Chris Mattison 137bc; David T. Grewcock 97cra; E & D Hosking 116bl; M.J.Thomas 97tr; P.A. Hayes 42–43; Roger Wilmshurst 81cb, 99cl; Silvestris 80bc. **Nancy Gardiner**: design Patrick Watson 20c, 24tr, 62–63 /design Felicity Flint 142–143, 143crb /design Mr & Mrs R Saunders 164. **Garden Picture Library**: Gary Rogers 29tr, 161bc; Henk Dijkman 98br, 136br, 183cr; J.S.Sira 71bc; John Glover 4fl col(iii), 5fr col(iii), 57tl, 91tr, 112bl; Kate Zari Roberts 154–155; Kim Beaxland front jacket br; Marijke Heuff back jacket cr, Mel Watson back jacket crb; Michelle Lamontagne 98bl; Morley Read 111br; Rex Butcher back jacket bl; Ron Sutherland 181tr; Steve Wooster 41cr; John Neubauer/design Oehme & van Sweden 88–89 **Garden Matters**: 155tr. **H. Gildemiester, Spain**: 142c, 142cb. **John Glover**: 4fl col(i), 5fr col(i), 56tl, 78–79, 79cl., (Derek Jarman) 60bl, 60cl. **Georgia Glynn-Smith**: 45cr, 96c, 111tl. **Isabelle Greene**: 66ca, 66cra. **Mick Hales, Green World Pictures**: design Jens Jensen 8tl, 16. **Janis Hall**: 9cl, 9tl, 22cb, 30bl, 38bl, 41br. **Gil Hanly**: design Gary Boyle 44–45c, /owner J. Gibbs/design Rod Barnett 165 cr. **Robert Harding Picture Library**: Adam Woolfitt 64bc; Advertasia Co. Ltd 158br; Brian Hawkes 80cb; Ian A. Griffiths 64cra; 65crb, 80crb; Luca Invernizzi Tettoni 158bl; Tom Macke 111tr. **Robert Harding Syndication**: Rob Judges /Homes & Gardens 46–47c. **Dennis Hardley Photography**: 178crb, 178br, 179br. **Jerry Harpur**: Arabella Lennox-Boyd 71ar 20 /design John Brookes (owners Julian & Marilyn Mulville, Argentina)

25cl, 31tr, 120tr, 120cr, 120bc, 121tl, 121tr, 121cr, 121br /Coton Manor Gardens, Northants 81bc /Edwina von Gal, New York 118 /design Sonny Garcia, San Francisco 165bc /design Oehme & van Sweden back jacket tr, 20, (owner Corbin Gwaltney) 31crb, (owner Michael Robinson) 21r /Richard Tan, Singapore 154cl. **Marijke Heuff**: design Gilles Clement 90bl, 90cl. **Holt Studios International**: Willem Harinck 119br.**Hutchison Library**: Dr. Nigel Smith 91br. **Image Bank**: Grant V. Faint 104crb. **The Irish Picture Library**: back inside flap bcl, 54bl, 65cr. **Gill Kenny**: 131, 132bl. **Carol Knoll**: design Patrick Watson front jacket tr, 30c, 128–129, 130cl. **David Lamb**: 50bl, 162tr. **Andrew Lawson**: 8br, 38c, 47tl, 79bc, /Augsburg Botanic Gardens, Germany 47tr /courtesy Miriam Rothschild 78br, 78bl, 79cr, 79tr /design Dan Pearson 162–163 /design Mirabel Osler 49tr /Docton Mill, Hartland, Devon 92bl, 93cl, 93cr, 93cb /Vann, Surrey 101clb, /West Park, Munich, Germany 21bl. **Tim Laws Macaire Photographic Bureau**: courtesy Mr & Mrs E.K. Bourcier 92–93, 93tr. **Allan Mandell**: 104cb. **Simon McBride**: 143cr. **Lisa Mierop**: 25tr, 94tr, 94cl, 94bc, 95tr, 95cr, 95br. **Linny Morris Cunningham**: front inside tl /design May Moir 25bl, 155br, 156tr, 156bc, 156cr, 157tr, 157bl, 157br. **Nature Photographers**: E.A. Janes 27bl. **N.H.P.A**: Alberto Nardi 88bl; David Woodfall 179ca; E. A. Janes 179 tr,; John Shaw 28 –29a. **Oxford Scientific Films**: 154bl; G. I. Bernard 151cl; Harold Taylor 159cr; Jack Dermid 160c; Max Gibbs 152b; Mark Hamblin 96ca; P. K. Sharpe 115br; Richard Davies 150br; Richard Packwood 130bc; Robert C. Nunnington 128bl; Ronald Toms 9bl, 48bl; Scott Camazine 161bl. **Planet Earth Pictures**: Alain Dragesco 130cra; J Eastcott & Y. Momatiuk 22bl, 124 cb, 124–125, Jan Tove Johansson 10cb; John Lythgoe front inside tc, 119cr. **Howard Rice**: 4fl col(ii), 5fr col(ii), 14l, 14–15, 15r, 27cr, 56tr, 64crb /design John Brookes 76tr, 76c, 77tc, 87cl, 87cr. **Felix Rigau**: design Isabelle Greene 41tr. **Gary Rogers**: back jacket cl, 138cl, 165tr. **Derek St Romaine**: front inside c, (design Bonita Bulaitis) 36–37, 46tr, 71cr /design Bonita Bulaitis 172bc, 172r, 172cl, 173tc, 173cr, 173br. **Susan A. Roth**: 29ca, 104cl, 124tr, 130tr, (design Neil Diboll) 119tr. **Vivien Russell**: design Nicole de Vésian front inside tr, 4fl col(vii), 5fr col(vii), 24br, 29cb, 56bl, 144bc, 144–145, 144–145c, 145tc, 146tr, 146bc, 147tl, 147tr, 147bl, 147br. **Sealand Aerial Photography Ltd**: 26–27c. **Harry Smith Collection**: 4tr, 4fl col(v), 5fr col(v), 56cr, 127bc, 160bc, 161clb. **The Stock Market**: 4fl col(viii), 5fr col(viii), 56br. **Tony Stone Images**: G. Ryan & S. Beyer 111bl; Gary Moon 137cr; Glen Allison 159ca /Liz Hymans 137cra; Martin Becka 158bc; Robin Smith 149cr. **James A. van Sweden**: design Oehme & van Sweden 4fl col(ix), 5fr col(ix), 42br, 57bl, 166bl, 167cr, 167bc, 167tr. **Werner Forman Archive**: Piers Morris Collection, London 124cl. **Peter Newark's Western Americana**: 124clb. **Elizabeth Whiting & Associates**: Gary Chowanetz 96bl, Karl-Dietrich Buhler 8cl, 36bl, 39cr, (design Nils Tomer) 12, 13r, Michael Dunne 140–141, Neil Lorimer 66bl. **Steve Wooster**: design John Brookes 6–7, 10–11 /Thijsse Park 17bl, 17br /design Piet Oudolf 18/ design Ton ter Linden 19 /design Henk Gerritsen 25tl /design John Brookes 34–35 /Thijsse Park 45br /design Ton ter Linden 50–51 /design John Brookes 53 /design Ton ter Linden 68–69 /design John Brookes 70 /design Henk Gerritsen 72–73c, 72bl, 72–73, 73ac, 74cl, 74bc, 74cr, 75bl, 75br /Thijsse Park 104cr, 105 /design Ton ter Linden 114l /design John Brookes 116–117, 162b, 165cl. **Michael S. Yamashita**: 13tl, 13tr.

BIBLIOGRAPHY

GENERAL

The American Horticultural Society A-Z Encyclopedia of Garden Plants; Dorling Kindersley, 1997.

RHS Plant Finder 1997-98; Dorling Kindersley, 1997.

Robinson, Peter, *The American Horticultural Society Complete Guide to Water Gardening*; Dorling Kindersley, 1997

BRITAIN

Brookes, Alan, *Woodlands: A Practical Handbook*; The British Trust for Conservation Volunteers, 1980.

Chambers, John, *Wild Flower Gardening*; Ward Lock Ltd, 1989.

Common Ground, The: The History, Evolution and Future of Britain's Countryside; Hutchinson & Co., 1980.

Fortey, Richard, *The Hidden Landscape: A Journey into the Geological Past*; Jonathan Cape, 1993.

Garton, Kate, Rothschild, Miriam, and de Rothschild, Lionel, *The Rothschild Gardens*; Gaia Books Ltd, 1996.

Harper, Peter, with Light, Jeremy, and Madsen, Chris, *The Natural Garden Book: Gardening in Harmony with Nature;* Gaia Books Ltd, 1994.

Jill, Duchess of Hamilton, *Scottish Plants for Scottish Gardens*; H.M Stationery Office

Kingsbury, Noel, *The New Perennial Garden*; Frances Lincoln, 1996.

Patchwork Landscape, The; The Reader's Digest Association, 1984.

Sand Dunes: A Practical Handbook; The British Trust for Conservation Volunteers, 1979.

Stevens, John, *The National Trust Book of Wild Flower Gardening*; Dorling Kindersley, 1987.

CONTINENT

Leopold, Rob, *Nature & Garden Art*; 1996.

Stationen in der StadtLandschaft; Perennials Perspectives, Creative Ecology and Integral Landscape Design, Srnheim Symposium, June 1996.

UNITED STATES

Ausubel, Kenny, *Seeds of Change: The Living Treasure*; Harper, 1994.

Bye, A. E., in *Abstracting the Landscape,* edited by Catherine Howett; The Department of Landscape Architecture, The Pennsylvania State University, 1990.

Druse, Ken, *The Natural Garden*; Clarkson Potter, 1989.

Druse, Ken, with Roach, Margaret, *The Natural Habitat Garden*; Clarkson Potter, 1994.

Francis, Mark, and Hester Jr., Randolph T. (eds), *The Meaning of Gardens*; MIT Press, 1990.

Gardening with Wildflowers and Native Plants; Brooklyn Botanic Garden, Inc., 1989.

Going Native: Biodiversity in Our Own Backyards; Brooklyn Botanic Garden, Inc., 1994.

Native Perennials; Brooklyn Botanic Garden, Inc., 1996.

Natural Lawn and Alternatives, The; Brooklyn Botanic Garden, Inc., 1993.

Ottesen, Carole, *The Native Plant Primer*; Harmony Books, 1995.

Ottesen, Carole, *The New American Garden*; Macmillan Publishing, 1987.

Pavlik, Bruce M., with Muick, Pamela C., Johnson, Sharon G., and Popper, Marjorie, *Oaks of California*; California Press, 1991.

AUSTRALIA

Smith, Bernard, with Smith, Terry, *Australian Painting 1788-1990*; Oxford University Press, 1991.

Snape, Diana, *Australian Native Gardens*; Lothian Publishing Co. Ltd, 1992.

Vandenbeld, John, *Nature of Australia*; Collins, 1988.

SOUTH AFRICA

Huntley, Brian J. (ed), with the assistance of Gelderblom, Caroline, and du Plessis, Emsie, *Botanical Diversity in Southern Africa*; National Botanical Institute, 1994.

TROPICAL

Warren, William, *The Tropical Garden*; Thames & Hudson, 1991.